Marx and the Proletariat

Contributions in Political Science
Series Editor: **BERNARD K. JOHNPOLL**

Marx and the Proletariat

A Study in Social Theory

Timothy McCarthy

CONTRIBUTIONS
IN POLITICAL SCIENCE,
NUMBER 18

Greenwood Press
Westport, Connecticut • London, England

Library of Congress Cataloging in Publication Data

McCarthy, Timothy, 1940-
    Marx and the proletariat.

    (Contributions in political science ; no. 18
ISSN 0147-1066)
    Bibliography: p.
    Includes index.
    1. Communism.   2. Dictatorship of the proletariat.
3. Historical materialism.   I. Title.   II. Series.
HX56.M23   335.4   78-4025
ISBN 0-313-20412-8

Library of Congress Catalog Card Number: 78-4025
ISBN: 0-313-20412-8
ISSN: 0147-1066

First published in 1978

Greenwood Press, Inc.
51 Riverside Avenue, Westport, Connecticut 06880

Printed in the United States of America

10 9 8 7 6 5 4 3 2 1

To
My Father and Mother

Contents

Preface

In this study I have taken seriously Marx's claim to have developed a theory of "scientific socialism"—scientific as distinct from utopian, or from the merely moral and philosophical. In other words, I have not followed the neorevisionist view, according to which the true Marx is revealed in the early writings. At the same time I have not taken the scientific claims of the mature Marx at their face value. What individuals say about themselves (as Marx was well aware) must be taken as a datum but not as the final word.

On a somewhat related point, I have not subscribed to the now fashionable thesis that Engels distorted, vulgarized, or somehow misrepresented the historical Marx. Forty years of the closest collaboration uniquely qualified Engels as an interpreter of Marx's intentions. While Engels's contributions to Marxism were decidedly less original and profound than those of Marx, there is no reason to suppose that they were any less authentic or authoritative. Consequently, I have not scrupled to cite Engels as speaking for Marx whenever it seemed convenient or necessary to do so.

I wish to point out that this study is in the form of an
"immanent critique." This means that I have sought to test
not the theory itself—historical materialism and the theory of
surplus value, and so forth—but to determine whether, given
these theoretical constructions, Marx's case for the revolutionary proletariat makes internal sense. In no way should it be
assumed that this purely methodological constraint implies
that I regard either Marx's historical or his economic theories
as adequate in themselves. In fact, I do not.

The work, in its original form, owes much to the good coun-
sel of Professors Heinz Lubasz and Gerald Izenberg. I wish to
take this opportunity to thank them for their invaluable help.

I would also like to express my gratitude to several of my
colleagues at the University of Massachusetts, Boston. Professor
Paul A. Gagnon read the original manuscript and encouraged
me to revise it for publication. Professor Richard H. Powers
read the revised manuscript and made some helpful comments
and suggestions. The final manuscript was read by Professor
Frances Malino, whose comments were, as always, valuable.

Professor Bernard Johnpoll has provided me with construc-
tive editorial advice, for which I am deeply grateful. To David
Nichols, Professor of Political Science at SUNY, Albany, I owe
a special note of thanks. He was instrumental in securing the
acceptance of my manuscript for publication.

Cambridge, Massachusetts
January 1978

Acknowledgments

International Publishers has kindly permitted me to quote from the following works: Karl Marx, *Capital* 1 (Moscow: Foreign Languages Publishing House, 1962); Karl Marx, *Class Struggles in France* (New York: International Publishers, 1964); Karl Marx, *The Eighteenth Brumaire of Louis Bonaparte* (New York: International Publishers, 1967); Karl Marx, *The Poverty of Philosophy* (Moscow: Foreign Languages Publishing House, no date); Karl Marx and Frederick Engels, *Selected Correspondence* (Moscow: Foreign Languages Publishing House, no date); and Karl Marx and Frederick Engels, *Selected Works*, 2 vols. (Moscow: Foreign Languages Publishing House, 1962). My thanks go also to Pitman Publishing Ltd., London, for permission to quote from *Karl Marx: Early Writings*, trans. T. B. Bottomore (London: C. A. Watts and Co., Ltd., 1963). Quotations from George Lichtheim, *Marxism: An Historical and Critical Study* (New York: Praeger, 1963) appear by permission of Praeger Publishers, Inc., a division of Holt, Rinehart, and Winston.

Introduction

The problem of the gap between theory and practice—more specifically, the failure of the proletariat to carry out its revolutionary mission—is as old as Marxism itself. The proletariat of 1848 fell far short of the historic role Marx had envisaged for it; the "revolutionary proletariat" of the Paris Commune was more a fiction of Marx's imagination than a historical reality. As early as the Marx-Bakunin controversy during the climactic years of the International, the Russian anarchist leader had accused Marx of allying himself with bourgeois and respectable (that is, nonrevolutionary) workers and turning his back upon the real revolutionary agents (landless peasants, artisans, the urban subproletariat). Although by the 1880s Marxist parties had been formed in most European countries, events soon showed that these parties were only nominally revolutionary while in practice reformist. The Revisionism which erupted in the Marxist movement around 1900 was explicitly based upon the premise that Marx's concept of the revolutionary proletariat was out of date. Even Lenin, while rehabilitating the revolutionary mission of the proletariat against the Revisionists, was careful to "revise" Marx in his own way: the working class by itself can attain only trade-union consciousness; revolutionary consciousness must be inculcated from without by a vanguard party composed chiefly of intellectuals. The disillusionment with Marxism in the West in the 1950s was not even dispelled by that paradoxical movement known as the New Left, which sprang up in the 1960s. On the contrary, one can say that the

basic presupposition of this movement was that the industrial
working class had become politically a spent force in all developed Western countries and indeed even a major prop of the
Establishment.

It has been the practice among Marxists and many non-
Marxists to explain this perennial gap between Marxian theory
and proletarian practice as a result of changing historical conditions. It is said, for example, that in 1848 European capitalism was not yet "ripe" for socialist revolution. Others say that
it is precisely in such conditions of "unripeness"—the crisis
years of early industrialization—that Marxian revolution has a
chance of success. But, the argument continues, when the
crisis years have passed (as they did in England after about
1850) the specter of proletarian revolution dissolves and gives
way to a reformist labor movement and democratic socialism.
More orthodox Marxists (including Leninists) see this capitalist
consolidation as made possible by imperialist expansion abroad
and attribute the loss of proletarian élan to the corrupting influence of imperialist superprofits and cheap colonial food-
stuffs. Surely all these arguments can be debated, but the one
thing which is taken for granted is that Marx was correct in
viewing the proletariat as a revolutionary class. Accepting that,
the task becomes one of explaining why history has nowhere
borne him out. An equally—and I would argue, more—compel-
ling explanation of these facts might be that there was something inherently wrong with Marx's concept of the revolutionary proletariat from the very beginning. This approach has
not been followed because it seems to go against one of the
principal claims of Marxism to be a "scientific" interpretation
of history and society. Hence if Marx was wrong he must have
been wrong on *empirical* grounds—wrong because he under-
estimated certain recuperative trends in capitalism, exaggerated
the trend toward increasing misery of the masses, ignored the
phenomenon of the new middle class, and so on. But suppose
one does not take Marx at his word; suppose one calls into
question the empirical, scientific character of his theory: one
is then free to entertain the heretical hypothesis that Marx did
not discover, but "invented" the revolutionary proletariat.[1]
This study attempts to substantiate that hypothesis.

Marx and the Proletariat

The Origins of Marx's Concept of the Revolutionary Proletariat, 1843-1845

Chapter 1

It is generally taken for granted that the foundations of Marx's concept of the revolutionary proletariat were his materialist conception of history and his critical political economy. Hence it is assumed that Marx, after extensive historical and economic study, was compelled to conclude that the proletariat is and must be a revolutionary class. This portrait of Marx as empiricist, however, accords very ill with the historical record. Marx first formulated his concept of the revolutionary proletariat in an essay begun in September 1843 and published in February 1844—a time when he had not yet formulated his materialist conception of history (this dates from 1845) and when he knew virtually nothing of economics. In fact, he reached his conclusions about the revolutionary character of the proletariat entirely as a result of his efforts to solve the problem of human alienation as posed by the Young Hegelians, notably Ludwig Feuerbach. More pointedly, Marx did not begin with the plight of the proletariat and then search for the means of its emancipation; rather he began with the question of how man could

be emancipated and saw in the proletariat the solution to the
problem.

It is important to reconstruct the process by which Marx
first arrived at and elaborated on his concept of the revolutionary proletariat. Because the theoretical impulse of Marx's development during this period (February 1843 to February
1845) comes from Feuerbach, this reconstruction must begin
with a brief consideration of the latter's intellectual contribution.

MARX'S FEUERBACHIAN CRITIQUE OF HEGEL

In his *Essence of Christianity* (1841), Feuerbach argued that
"religion has its basis in the essential difference between man
and the brute."[1] This essential difference consists in man's
consciousness of himself as a species(universal)-being, and not
merely as an individual. "Consciousness in the strictest sense is
present only in a being to whom his species, his essential nature,
is an object of thought."[2] Because man is conscious of himself
as a species-being, man is also conscious of the gap between the
potentialities of the species and the actual human individual.[3]
The individual man recognizes his limitations and deficiencies.
He can in fact imagine all the powers and faculties of man raised
to the level of ultimate perfection. But instead of recognizing
this image of human perfection as the product of his own imagination, he objectifies it; he makes it into a being external to
and independent of him—God. Feuerbach here was describing
the psychological mechanism of projection, according to which
human beings convert their own wishes into persons or things
which are outside themselves. These persons or things begin
to take on a life of their own; they come to dominate their
creators. They command, they prohibit, they punish. Indeed
so much is the original relation between man and God inverted
that man imagines that God created him and not he God.

This unconscious process of objectification has profound
consequences: the more men exalt God, the more they degrade
themselves. "In proportion as the divine subject is in reality
human, the greater is the apparent difference between God and
man; that is, the more . . . is the identity of the divine and the

human denied, and the human, considered as such, is depreciated. . . . To enrich God man must become poor; that God may be all, man must be nothing."[4] From this insight it is only a short step to recognizing that human misery and suffering is the breeding ground of religious faith: "The more empty life is, the fuller, the more concrete is God. The impoverishment of the real world and the enriching of God is one act. Only the poor man has a rich God."[5] Man enriches God to compensate for the inhumanity of his everyday life.

Feuerbach sees in the Christian notion of a life after death the same compensatory mechanism. "As God is nothing else than the nature of man purified from that which, to the human individual, appears, whether in feeling or in thought, as a limitation, an evil; so the future life is nothing else than the present life freed from that which appears as a limitation or evil."[6] And again: "The future life is nothing else than life in unison with feeling, with the idea, which the present life contradicts. The whole import of the future life is the abolition of this discordance and the realization of a state which corresponds to the feelings in which man is in unison with himself."[7]

Man is in the process of remembering that he is God, that the divine is only the as-yet-unrealized potentialities of man.

> The necessary turning-point in history is therefore the *open confession* [italics mine] that the consciousness of God is nothing else than the consciousness of the species; that man can and should raise himself only above the limits of his individuality, and not above . . . the positive essential conditions of his species; that there is no other essence which man can think, dream of, imagine, feel, believe in, wish for, love and adore as the absolute than the essence of human nature itself.[8]

In short, the overcoming of religion is only a question of insight, of recognizing the human essence of the divine: we need only "invert the religious relations—regard that as an end which religion regards as a means—exalt that into the primary which in religion is subordinate, the accessory, the condition—*at once* we have destroyed the illusion, and the unclouded light of truth streams in upon us."[9]

In early 1843 (nearly two years after the publication of *Essence*) Feuerbach published his "Preliminary Theses on the Reform of Philosophy." In this work, which had a profound and direct influence on Marx, Feuerbach applied the same critical method he had used in analyzing religion to philosophy, particularly to Hegelian philosophy. Feuerbach contended that this application was entirely justified on the grounds that Hegelian philosophy was really crypto-religion and therefore a species of the same human self-alienation he had uncovered in his analysis of religion: Hegel had merely substituted Spirit (*Geist*), or the Idea, for God. It was this explosive insight which impelled Marx to break decisively with the Hegelian heritage (even in its "Left" version) and to begin a "Feuerbachian" critique of Hegel's political thought which led him to revolutionary communism. In view of the momentous implications of this intellectual revolution it is helpful to trace its development and main features.

It is often said that Marx turned Hegel "right side up," whereas before he had been "standing on his head." This image of "materializing" the Hegelian dialectic is appropriate to Marx's writings after 1845, but it is positively misleading when applied to his critical writings on Hegel during 1843-1844. Marx's basic criticism of Hegel at this point—and here we see the influence of Feuerbach—was that Hegel had transformed essential human attributes into an independent subject (Idea, Spirit) and had endowed this fantastic subject with the creative powers actually belonging to man himself. The central issue was first stated succinctly in Marx's unfinished draft of *A Critique of Hegel's Philosophy of Right* (spring-summer 1843). He writes:

If the modes of man's *social* existence, as found for example in the development of family, civil society, state, etc. are regarded as the actualization and objectification of man's *essence*, then family, civil society, etc. appear as qualities inhering in subjects. Man then remains what is essential within these realities, while these then appear as his actualized universality, and hence also as something common to all men.[10]

But if, on the contrary, Hegel's view is accepted, "family, civil society, the state, are determinants of the Idea, of substance as subject . . . they must *receive* [from the Idea] an empirical actuality, and the mass of men in which the idea of civil society is developed *takes on* the identity of citizen of civil society, and that in which the idea of the state is developed takes on that of citizen of the state."[11] In short, Hegel's fundamental error lay in conceiving of the essence of man as an independent subject, as the self-actualization of the Idea, instead of conceiving the human essence as the self-actualization and objectification of empirically existing, active men. Men create, produce their own essence ("man") through their practical activity: they themselves produce the human world—State, society, religion, art, science, morality.[12]

At this stage (1843) Marx had not clearly differentiated types and levels of human activity. In the *Critique*, family, civil society, and State are lumped together as the products of human activity, in opposition to the Hegelian thesis that they are the product of the activity of the Idea. However, by the time he wrote *The Jewish Question* (November 1843) the State had been relegated to the status of an illusory community relative to the "real life" of civil society. The State was still conceived as the product of human activity, indeed as an expression of the essence of man (species-being), but an essence in alienation from itself. As Marx saw it, in the fully democratic State man appeared as himself, as a communal being, but the State itself, political life, is a merely abstract, illusory realm; by contrast in real life, in civil society, man was the opposite of himself, a purely egoistic being. Thus true man is unreal and real man is untrue.

> Man as member of civil society is identified with authentic man, man as distinct from citizen, because he is man in his sensuous existence, whereas political man is only an abstract, artificial man, man as an allegorical, moral person. Thus man as he really is, is seen only in the form of egoistic man, and man in his true nature only in the form of the abstract citizen.[13]

In *The Jewish Question*, of course, Marx was criticizing the democratic State, the State in which all persons have (in theory) equal political rights, are all members of the sovereign people. In principle, then, the Hegelian dichotomy between civil society and the State has been broken down insofar as the individual has become both private person and political man. But Marx argued that, in fact, this only meant (as Hegel feared) the subjection of the State (the supposed communal life of man) to the egoism of civil society.

> The political liberators reduce citizenship, the political community, to a mere *means* for serving these so-called rights of man; and consequently . . . the citizen is declared to be the servant of egoistic "man," . . . the sphere in which man functions as a species-being is degraded to a level below the sphere where he functions as a political being, and finally . . . it is man as a *bourgeois* and not man as citizen who is considered the true and authentic man.[14]

Consequently, Marx concluded that political emancipation (as exemplified in the French Revolution) had not overcome the dualism of egoistic man and social man, but had merely raised this dualism to a new level of intensity and clarity.

> The perfected political state is, by its nature, the *species-life* of man as opposed to his material life. All the presuppositions of this egoistic life continue to exist in civil society outside of the political sphere as qualities of civil society. When the political state has attained to its full development, man leads not only in thought, in consciousness, but in reality, in life, a double existence—celestial and terrestrial. He lives in the political community where he regards himself as a communal being, and in civil society where he acts simply as a private individual, treats other men as means, degrades himself to a mere means, and becomes the plaything of alien powers.[15]

ECONOMICS AND ALIENATION

Prior to 1844 Marx's theory of alienation centered around the relationship between civil society and the State. Political life is seen as the illusory realization of man's essence (his communal being) in alienation from his real life. This line of argument entirely parallels Feuerbach's critique of religion; man realizes himself vicariously in God. But at this stage Marx's concept of man as a species-being goes little beyond the contrasting of communitarian and individualistic man. Society may have been defined as "real" vis-à-vis the State, but there is yet no effort to differentiate types and levels of activity within society itself. This differentiation comes only with the *Economic-Philosophical Manuscripts* of 1844, and here the theoretical impetus comes from Hegel rather than from Feuerbach.

In the 1844 *Manuscripts*, labor, that is, productive activity, becomes the central category of Marx's thought. At this juncture Hegelian philosophy and English political economy converge. For Marx the connection between these two seemingly disparate intellectual currents was that both (in their different ways) recognized labor as the paradigmatic human activity. Political economy saw labor as the essence of wealth;[16] Hegel saw labor (understood, to be sure, as abstract, intellectual labor) as the "self-creation of man."[17] The labor which man expends in the production of commodities is objectified in these commodities: the products of labor are the materialization, the sensuous embodiment, of the human essence. "Nature, as it develops in human history, in the act of genesis of human society, is the actual nature of man."[18] Or again: "The history of industry and industry as it objectively exists is an open book of the human faculties, and a human psychology which can be sensuously apprehended."[19] However, Marx goes on: "This history [of industry] has so far been conceived in relation to human nature only from a superficial utilitarian point of view, since in the condition of alienation it was only possible to conceive real human faculties and human species-action in the form of general human existence, as *religion*."[20]

But how can this be? What has prevented men from conceiving of their productive-life as species-life, their creations as self-creation, their objectified labor as objectified man? The realization of man in the object must at the same time be a loss of man, a loss of the object. It must no longer appear as belonging to him, but as something alien to him.

Marx begins his analysis with what he calls a "contemporary economic fact."[21] To paraphrase his more dramatic formulation of this "fact" in the prosaic language of political economy, the more the introduction of machinery and the extension of the division of labor enables the worker to produce, the more the worker's share in the total product of his labor decreases. The more machinery is introduced and production thereby increased, the more the price of labor (wages) is reduced, as a result of the competition among the workers for the diminished number of jobs. Finally, the more machinery is introduced and the scale of production thereby enlarged, the more small businessmen and artisans are driven into the proletariat, thus intensifying competition among the workers and further lowering their standard of living. The worker, therefore, is obliged to be his own gravedigger: the more goods he produces, the more competitors he produces in the form of fresh recruits to the ever-swelling army of the proletariat.

Now for Marx this fact (or rather, cluster of related facts) constitutes the structural basis of alienation: "It implies that the object produced by labor, its product, now stands opposed to it as an alien being, as a power independent of the producer."[22] The worker's life is dominated by forces beyond his control (by the natural laws of the free market), forces which drive him irresistibly, against his will but through his own agency, into deepening degradation and misery.

> The performance of work appears in the sphere of political economy as a vitiation of the worker, objectification as a loss and as servitude to the object, and appropriation as alienation. So much does the performance of work appear as vitiation that the worker is vitiated to the point of starvation. So much does objectification appear as loss of the object that the worker is deprived of the most essential things, not only of life but also of work. Labor itself becomes an object which he can acquire only by the greatest effort and with unpredictable interruptions. So much does the appropriation of the object appear as alienation that the more objects the worker produces the fewer he can pos-

sess and the more he falls under the domination of his product, of capital.[23]

As in Hegelian philosophy, the essence of man takes on an existence independent of man. "The life which he [the worker] has given to the object sets itself against him as an alien and hostile force."[24] More simply: "What is embodied in the object is no longer his own."[25]

But it is not only that the product of labor is alien to the worker; the worker has now come to view work, productive activity, as an activity alien to him, not part of his nature.

> The work is external to the worker . . . it is not part of his nature; and consequently he does not fulfill himself in his work but denies himself, has a feeling of misery rather than well-being, does not develop freely his mental and physical energies but is physically exhausted and mentally debased. The worker therefore feels himself at home only in his leisure time, whereas at work he feels homeless. His work is not voluntary but imposed, forced labor. It is not the satisfaction of a need but only a means for satisfying other needs. Its alien character is clearly shown by the fact that as soon as there is no physical or other compulsion it is avoided like the plague. External labor, labor in which man alienates himself, is a labor of self-sacrifice, of mortification.[26]

In his animal activities (sex, eating, drinking) the worker feels himself human, whereas in his truly human activity—labor—man is reduced to an animal.[27]

This last point leads directly into Marx's philosophical anthropology. Man distinguishes himself from the animals by his productive activity. Man is essentially a productive being. But it is not the mere fact of producing, but the nature and scope of his productive activity which sets him apart from animals.

> Of course, animals also produce. They construct nests, dwellings, as in the case of bees, beavers, ants, etc. But they only produce what is strictly necessary for themselves or their young. They produce only in a single direction, while man produces universally. They produce only under the compulsion of direct, physical needs, while man produces when he is free from

physical need and only truly produces in freedom from such
need.[28]

In other words, only that productive activity which is free,
that is, self-determined, done for its own sake, is truly human
activity. By this standard, alienated labor represents a total
reversal of the true relation between ends and means, essence
and existence. "For labor, life-activity, productive life, now
appears to man only as a means for the satisfaction of a need,
the need to maintain his physical existence."[29]

Another aspect of alienation is that man is alienated from
other men, that is, he stands in an alien relation to other men.
To understand this more clearly we must keep in mind Marx's
dictum that "the relation of man to himself is first realized,
objectified, through his relation to other men."[30] Hence man
can stand in an alien relation to himself only if he first stands
in an alien relation to other men.

> If he is related to the product of his labor, his objectified
> labor, as to an alien, hostile, powerful, and independent ob-
> ject, he is related in such a way that another alien, hostile, power-
> ful and independent man is the lord of his object. If he is related
> to his own activity as to unfree activity, then he is related to it
> as activity in the service, and under the dominion, coercion and
> yoke of another man.[31]

However, at the same time, through his own activity, "through
alienated labor, the worker creates the relation of another man,
who does not work and who is outside the work process, to
this labor. The relation of the worker to work also produces the
relation of the capitalist . . . to work. Private property is therefore the product, the necessary result of alienated labor."[32]
Thus not only does the worker alienate his own activity; he also
"bestows upon the stranger [the capitalist] an activity which
is *not his own.*"[33] (Italics mine.) In effect, then, both worker
and capitalist are alienated; both are forced into activities which
are not their own.

Several inferences may now be drawn: (1) Men are free only
when nothing is external to their will. The worker in modern
society is governed by forces external to his will (namely, the

products of his own labor which have been transformed into commodities) and therefore the worker is unfree. The alienation and private appropriation of the products of labor, therefore, is *slavery*. (2) The social division of labor (especially the lifelong enslavement to the machine) denies man's nature as a universal producer and therefore is *slavery*.[34] (3) Wage-labor (that is, working *only* to satisfy one's physical needs and not for the purpose of self-realization) is incompatible with man's character as a species-being, and therefore is *slavery*.[35] (4) Because bourgeois society is based upon self-interest (egoism), it violates man's truly social nature as a communal being and *enslaves* men to their appetites.[36] In bourgeois society men treat each other as means and not as ends.

Now few will grant that these propositions are self-evident. Moreover, many would find them baffling. If having nothing external to our will is freedom, freedom must be a rare thing indeed. But even granting the definition, how does the communal appropriation of the products of labor bring freedom? It does if one believes, with Rousseau, that the communal will is never external to the will of the individuals. Again, it is far from obvious that any society which does not require individuals to do all things is based on slavery, or that it is based on slavery if it does require individuals to do just one thing. In the same vein, it seems simply arbitrary to say that working for wages is in itself and necessarily an unfree activity. But this is precisely what Marx does say. Lastly, it may be wondered why a society which seeks to satisfy the needs of its members through the operation of self-interest (rather than, say, through altruistic appeals) is to be regarded as immoral, "selfish," and as leading to an enslavement to appetite—unless the unabashed acknowledgment of desires and needs is supposed to be itself immoral. That such a society may be less efficient or less equitable in satisfying needs is surely a relevant concern, but Marx's point (in the early writings) is addressed to neither the efficiency nor the equity but to the morality of a society organized around the principle of self-interest.

In raising these considerations I am not proposing to resolve the questions posed, but merely to suggest the blatantly a priori character of Marx's assumptions.

THE PROLETARIAT AND HUMAN EMANCIPATION

Marx's theory of alienation is a comprehensive analysis and indictment of the human condition in bourgeois society. While Marx underscores the particular degradation and dehumanization of the proletariat, it is clear that alienation is a condition which afflicts *all* members of bourgeois society, though not necessarily to the same degree. From this perspective, the proletariat represents only the most palpable and acute expression of a malaise which consumes everyone. The worker, for example, may be alienated from the product of his labor and from work itself, but the capitalist is also alienated from productive life altogether. The worker, through the division of labor, is enslaved to a machine, but the capitalist also suffers from the dwarfing, constricting, and fragmenting effects of the division of labor. The worker works merely in order to survive, but this is only a more brutalizing consequence of a general law, according to which all members of bourgeois society must sacrifice their need for self-realization to the need to "earn a living." Lastly, in a society which sees men merely as means, and merely as means to egoistic gratification, men can only see each other as means and not as ends. This alienation of "man from other men" is the common lot of worker and capitalist—though, again, not necessarily to the same degree or to the same effect.

How can alienation be overcome? This is Marx's answer:

> From the relation of alienated labor to private property it also follows that the emancipation of society from private property, from servitude, takes the political form of the emancipation of the workers; not in the sense that only the latter's emancipation is involved, but because this emancipation includes the emancipation of humanity as a whole. For all human servitude is involved in the relation of the worker to production, and all the types of servitude are only modifications or consequences of this relation.[37]

But if it is society at large—humanity as a whole—which is to be emancipated, why must the work of emancipation be the work of a particular class? And why is that particular class the proletariat rather than the capitalist class? Marx answers:

The propertied class and the class of the proletariat present
the same human self-alienation. But the former class finds in
this self-alienation its confirmation and its comfort, its own
power; it has in it a semblance of human existence. The class
of the proletariat feels annihilated in its own self-alienation;
it sees in it its own powerlessness and the reality of an inhuman
existence.[38]

The proletariat lacks "even the semblance of humanity."[39]
Curiously enough, it is precisely this total loss of humanity
which enables the proletariat to typify, represent, and redeem
man.

Since the conditions of life of the proletariat sum up all the
conditions of life of society today in all their inhuman acuity;
since man has lost himself in the proletariat, yet at the same
time has not only gained a theoretical consciousness of that
loss, but has been driven through urgent, unmistakable, absolutely pressing need—by practical necessity—to revolt against
that inhumanity.[40]

But in revolting against these "inhuman conditions," in seeking
to emancipate itself as a class, "it cannot abolish the conditions
of its own life without abolishing all the inhuman conditions of
life of society today, which are summed up in its own situation."[41] Thus the proletariat in seeking to emancipate itself (that
is, abolish the nexus of wage labor and private property) must
of necessity emancipate society as a whole (itself and the propertied class).

The proletariat, then, is a "universal class" because "its suf-
ferings are universal"[42]—because it represents the universal pre-
dicament of man, in present-day society, in its most drastic and
consummate form and because its own liberation as a class necessarily coincides with a universal liberation, the liberation of
man.

Marx's emphasis on the proletariat as a "total loss of humanity" and its role in the "total redemption of humanity"[43] is important. Only that class which has been completely stripped of
all humanity (even the semblance of humanity) can comprehend

the real meaning of that loss and the true meaning of its humanity. Only such a class has the vital need to be human; only such
a class is denied the comfort of illusions. Indeed, Marx seems to
accord to this "human consciousness" a decisive role in revolutionary practice when he speaks of the proletariat as "that misery
conscious of its physical and spiritual misery, that dehumanization conscious of its dehumanization, and *therefore self-abolish-
ing.*"[44] (Italics mine) By contrast, the consciousness of the propertied class is dulled, deceived, and obscured by its relative
well-being (the semblance of a human existence). The proletariat then, in representing the *real interest* of man (identical
with its own interest as class) necessarily represents the *real interest* of the propertied class over and against their *apparent*
interest as a class.

In conclusion, Marx's concept of the revolutionary proletariat,
as formulated in the early writings, rests entirely on the theory
of alienation, which in turn rests upon his concept of human
nature (man as universal producer, as social being). If it is agreed
that Marx's philosophical anthropology is based on a priori assumptions, it follows that the inferences drawn from these assumptions must have the same character. In short, Marx did not
base his view of the proletarian mission on empirical grounds,
but derived it from the a priori concepts of his philosophical
anthropology.[45]

THE THEORY OF REVOLUTION

Marx's concept of human nature formed the basis of his
revolutionary theory. Using Germany as a focus, it is possible
to see how Marx applied his revolutionary theory in specific
historical situations.

In the 1844 *Manuscripts* Marx points out that the historical
movement toward communism has "different beginnings" in
different countries, "according to whether the actual and established life of the people is more in the realm of mind or more
in the external world, is real or ideal life."[46] For example, in
Germany, where religion (ideal life) still dominates, communism
begins as atheism: the negation of the existence of God is the
abstract affirmation of the existence of man. In France, on the

other hand, where politics is dominant, communism begins as the abstract demand for equality.[47] (Proudhon is singled out for criticism in this connection.) Only in England is communism grounded in real life—in "real, material, self-sufficient, practical need."[48] In other words, only in England (as of 1844) had the critique of alienation assumed a clear economic form.

Marx's general theory of alienation thus enabled him to link together, in developmental terms, the historical situations of the three major European countries—to fuse German philosophy, French socialism, and English political economy. However, the linking together of these three countries also implied something about the probable course of their revolutionary development. On the face of it, one would assume that England would be the first country to establish communism, France the next (but only after superceding its political fetishism), and Germany the last, since it had not yet even reached the political stage prevalent in France. But Marx, at this stage (1843-1844) still a German revolutionary, could hardly be expected to content himself with the gradualist implications of his own theory with regard to Germany. A basis must be found within the theory itself for revolutionary communist action in Germany.

Marx set the stage for his justification of imminent communist revolution in Germany by pointing to certain peculiarities of Germany's historical development. Since the Reformation, Germany had been historically stagnant: England and France had experienced political revolutions and social upheaval, while Germany remained fixated at the threshold of the modern world. The active element of German history was banished to the realm of thought: German philosophy was "the ideal prolongation of German history."[49] In this philosophical fantasy world Germans thought what other nations had done.[50] Germany reproduced in the realm of abstraction the actual historical process going on in Western Europe. Thus, while Germany had not yet even emancipated itself from the Middle Ages, it was already the philosophical contemporary of the most advanced European nations.[51] That is, German philosophy (via Hegel and Feuerbach) had already reached communism—though still in an abstract form. The Germans had al-

ready superceded the present stage of Western nations in
thought and had already reached the stage which would be
their immediate future.

However, Marx clearly realized that philosophy by itself
could not change existing political and social conditions in
Germany. Philosophy must become "practical," that is, discover a "weapon," a "material basis," in order to realize itself.
This force Marx saw in the proletariat.

But how could Marx believe that the German proletariat,
admittedly just in the process of formation, would be able
to make a communist revolution in a politically and industrially backward country? Marx's answer to this entirely appropriate
question centered on two considerations. The first was the belief that the German bourgeoisie was incapable of making a
revolution in the manner of their French counterparts. This,
however, did not prove that the proletariat would be any more
capable: indeed it more nearly proved that not even a bourgeois revolution was possible for Germany. Second, it was precisely because Germany was politically backward that the proletariat would make a communist revolution.[52] This remarkable
conclusion can be derived from Marx's theory of alienation—
from the "reality" of the social (human) as contrasted with the
illusoriness of the political. As Marx had observed:

> The more developed and general the political intelligence of
> a people is, the more the proletariat—at least at the beginning
> of the movement—wastes its energies in irrational and useless
> uprisings which are suppressed in blood. Because it thinks po-
> litically, it sees the cause of all social evils in will and all remedies
> in force and the overthrow of a particular form of state. As
> evidence, consider the first outbreak of the French proletariat.
> The workers of Lyon believed they were pursuing political
> aims, that they were only soldiers of the Republic, while actually
> they were the soldiers of socialism. Thus their political
> understanding clouded the roots of their social misery,
> distorted their insight into their actual aims, and deceived
> their social instinct.[53]

The German proletariat, it seems, would fortunately not be
encumbered by the smoke screen of political illusions, but

would see clearly the social roots of its misery and act according-
ly. Marx was convinced by the Silesian weavers' revolt of 1844
that this was already happening.

> Not a single French and English labor revolt possessed such a
> theoretical and conscious character as the rising of the Silesian
> weavers. . . . The Silesian uprising begins exactly where the French
> and English labor revolts end, with the consciousness of the nature
> of the proletariat. The action itself bears this superior character.
> Not only the machines, the rivals of the workers, are destroyed,
> but also account books and titles of property. While all other
> movements were directed against the visible enemy, the indus-
> trial lord, this movement is at the same time directed against the
> hidden enemy, the banker.[54]

Thus, at Marx's hands, the political backwardness of Germany
is magically transformed from a disadvantage to a positive
virtue. This theoretical tour de force, while it rescued him from
one awkward conclusion, immediately confronted him with
another. In the context of the German political scene in 1843-
1844, it meant urging the proletariat not to collaborate with the
bourgeoisie in the "merely" political struggle then shaping up
against absolutism. Ultimately, Marx's formulation of the theory
of historical materialism after 1845 led him to abandon this
earlier ultraradicalism, inasmuch as he came to accept the necessity of bourgeois revolution in Germany (though it would serve
only as the prelude to proletarian-communist revolution) and
of the alliance of the proletariat with the bourgeoisie in the
struggle against absolutism.

   Therefore, it may be concluded that Marx in his writings of
1843-1844 assigned a uniquely important role to philosophy as
a catalyst of the revolutionary process. But, as I have suggested,
Marx saw this as a uniquely German phenomenon, reflecting the
peculiarities of German historical development.

> The emancipation of Germany is only possible *in practice* if one
> adopts the point of view of that theory according to which man
> is the highest being for man. . . . The emancipation of Germany
> will be an emancipation of man. Philosophy is the *head* of this
> emancipation and the proletariat is its *heart*. Philosophy can only

be realized by the abolition of the proletariat and the proletariat
can only be abolished by the realization of philosophy.[55]

Marx nowhere in these early writings suggests a comparable role
for philosophy in France or England. Rather he seems to have
envisaged a kind of international division of labor within the
European proletariat, in which the proletariat of each country
developed a distinctive character and contribution based upon
the special conditions of its national history. The German proletariat—reflecting Germany's philosophical "specialization"— is
the theorist of the European proletariat, just as the English proletariat is its economist and the French proletariat its politician.[56]
We must therefore conclude that the alliance of philosophy and
the proletariat was seen by Marx as a purely local event, or
rather a local variant of a general European process, and in no
sense the cornerstone of even his early revolutionary theory
taken as a whole.

CONCLUSION

The most critical implications of Marx's concept of the revolutionary proletariat can be summarized as follows:

(1) Marx began with the problem of human emancipation
and found in the proletariat a solution to that problem.

(2) Marx derived his belief in the revolutionary mission of
the proletariat from the a priori assumptions of his philosophical
anthropology and not from empirical analysis.

(3) In identifying the proletariat with man and the emancipation of the proletariat with the emancipation of man, Marx
established the proletariat as the representative of the true interest of man, of society as a whole—including the propertied
class. The ambiguity in this conception—the tension between
the universalism of the ends (human emancipation) and the
particularism of the means (the emancipation of a class)— will
be explored further.

(4) Communism, far from being a "class doctrine," is simply
the theory and practice of human emancipation. Communism
is "the positive abolition of private property, of human self-
alienation, and thus the real appropriation of human nature by

and for man. It is, therefore, the return of man to himself as a social, i.e., really human being, a complete and conscious return which assimilates all the wealth of previous development."[57]

(5) The consciousness of the proletariat is not a class consciousness, but a human consciousness—a recognition of the absolute contradiction between human nature (essence) and the conditions of life in bourgeois society (existence). This consciousness, potentially common to all members of society, is actualized fully only in the proletariat.

Historical
Materialism
Chapter 2

Marx's method in the early writings was to postulate an ideal "human essence" (a universal human nature) and to show that in existing society man lives in contradiction to his essence, lives a "false" existence. Religion, State, law, morality, philosophy are seen as manifestations of this anomalous condition, that is, as forms of alienation. The concept of the revolutionary proletariat is deduced from the doctrine of alienation, which in turn presupposes the notion of a human essence. After 1845 Marx adopted a radically different method: He explicitly rejected "philosophy" in favor of "positive science,"[1] which implied an empirical approach to the study of society qualitatively different from the former normative-deductive one. Among other things this change involved the study of *men* as they actually exist under different material conditions of life, that is, under different social relations of production and different levels of technology.[2] It involved a theory of historical causation and a theory of ideology, according to which religion, State, law, morality, and philosophy are no longer regarded as the manifestations of an inauthentic existence in conflict with the true nature of man, but as forms of consciousness determined by the specific economic structure of society. By the same token, the case for the revolutionary proletariat was no longer made on the basis of a human consciousness, but on the basis of an empirically determined class consciousness.[3]

The significance and implications of these changes in Marx's thought make it necessary to explicate the principal tenets of historical materialism. Beginning with the most general statement of the theory—that of the 1859 Preface to the *Contribution to a Critique of Political Economy*—the exposition will then examine the refinements of this general theory in Marx's historical studies, notably the *Eighteenth Brumaire of Louis Bonaparte*.

The materialist conception of history was originally formulated in conscious opposition to the Hegelian conception of history. Whereas Marx and Hegel agreed that there was a definite correlation between the material and spiritual development of mankind, they understood the nature of this connection in radically different ways. As Marx was to observe in his preface to *Capital*,

My dialectic method is not only different from the Hegelian but is its direct opposite. To Hegel, the life-processes of the human brain, i.e., the process of thinking, which under the name of the "Idea" he even transformed into an independent subject, is the demiurgos of the real world and the real world is only the existent phenomenal form of the "Idea." With me, on the contrary, the ideal is nothing else than the material world reflected by the human mind and translated into forms of thought.[4]

From this general methodological precept it is an easy transition to the more concrete formulations of the 1859 "Preface":

In the social production which men carry on they enter into definite relations which are indispensable and independent of their will; these relations of production correspond to a definite stage of development of their material powers of production. The sum total of these relations of production constitutes the economic structure of society—the real foundation, on which

rise legal and political superstructures and to which correspond
definite forms of social consciousness. The mode of production
in material life determines the general character of the social,
political, and spiritual processes of life. It is not the consciousness of men that determines their existence, but, on the contrary, their social existence determines their consciousness.[5]

In this passage Marx maintains that the social relations of
production (which seem to be synonymous with "property
relations") *correspond* to a "definite stage" of development
of the "material powers of production." This last phrase is
somewhat general, but Marx seems to mean by it primarily
technology. The notion, however, that social relations of
production "correspond" with the stage of development of
the material powers of production leaves unclear what
causal connection there might be between them. In spite of
aphorisms to the effect that the handmill created the feudal
lord and steam power the industrial capitalist, it seems unlikely
that Marx held the view that technology *determined* the social
relations of production. At most he seems to have viewed the
level of technology at any given time as an "indication"—no
more—of the "social conditions under which labor is carried
on."[6] But whatever the precise relation between technology
and social relations of production, it is clear that the latter
constitute the *real basis* upon which the legal and political
"superstructure" *arises* and *to which correspond* "definite
forms of social consciousness." Thus law and political forms
arise from the social relations of production, whereas the forms
of social consciousness (religion, philosophy, morality, art) are
said to correspond to these same social relations of production.
This formulation suggests that the relation between social relations of production and ideologies is far less direct than that between social relations of production and the legal-political superstructure. Why this should be so is not made clear, but it may
be supposed that law and political structures are for Marx more
closely associated with production than are religious, philosophical, moral, and esthetic ideas.

The main point, however, is Marx's assertion that the mode
of production determines the "general character" of the "social,

political, and spiritual processes of life." By this he seems to mean that the forms which the latter assume are most appropriate and ideally suited to the requirements of the particular system of material production. For example, Marx believed that the democratic republic was the *logical form* of bourgeois rule, that is, the *typical* political form of mature capitalism. Similarly, he believed that Protestantism was the religion most appropriate to and reflective of the capitalist mode of production.

> The religious world is but a reflex of the real world. And for a society based on the production of commodities, in which the producers in general enter into relations with one another by treating their products as commodities and values, whereby they reduce their individual private labor to the standard of homogeneous human labor—for such a society Christianity with its cult of abstract man, more especially in its bourgeois developments, Protestantism, Deism, etc. is the most fitting form of religion.[7]

Thus Marx is saying that given a knowledge of the "actual relations of life at any given time" (that is, the social relations of production) it should be possible to infer from these the "corresponding 'spiritualized' forms."[8]

Let us now turn to Marx's theory of social change as elaborated in the same text:

> At a certain stage of their development, the material forces of production in society come in conflict with the existing relations of production, or—what is but a legal expression for the same thing—with the property relations within which they had been at work before. From forms of development of the forces of production these relations turn into their fetters. Then comes the period of social revolution. With the change of the economic foundation the entire immense superstructure is more or less rapidly transformed.[9]

In this passage Marx is surprisingly vague about the nature of the social revolution. We hear nothing about class struggle or class-consciousness. Indeed one is left with the impression that the change in the social relations of production (which is the

practical meaning of social revolution) occurs simply as a result
of the insistent urgings of the productive forces. Perhaps Marx
thought that this was ultimately the case, but it is odd to find
no mention here of the fact that the antagonism between forces
of production and social relations of production must be reflected in an antagonism between classes, and that it is this conflict which constitutes the motor force of social change. That
Marx omits this from his account may be due, in part, to the
high level of abstraction at which he is operating, or to his con-
fidence in the inexorability of the historical laws which he had
uncovered—or both. At any rate, the social revolution, once carried through, brings into being new social relations of production,
which make possible the full utilization of the productive forces
of society and upon which arise (with allowance for a certain
amount of cultural lag) a new legal and political superstructure
and to which correspond (again allowing for some historical
inertia) new ideological forms.

Marx goes on to develop a theory of conscious and unconscious motivation in history. In periods of social transformation men become conscious of the real conflicts in material life
only indirectly and in inverted form—as ideological conflict, as
the conflict between political or religious ideas. The real basis
of their action, their real motives, remain unknown to them.

> Just as our opinion of an individual is not based on what he
> thinks of himself, so we cannot judge of such an era of trans-
> formation by its own consciousness; on the contrary, this
> consciousness must rather be explained in terms of the contra-
> dictions of material life, from the existing conflict between the
> social forces of production and the relations of production.[10]

The contradictions which emerge at the ideological level are
only the expression (or symptom) of the contradictions in
material life. For example, the Enlightenment (by Marx's account) was merely the symptom of that crisis in French society
which was resolved in the Revolution of 1789.

Now if one believes that social change is a lawfully determined process, and specifically if one believes that Marx dis-
covered these laws, then it follows that social change is not so

much a matter of human will as it is a matter of the ripeness of historical conditions. This was indeed Marx's view.

> No social order ever disappears before all the productive forces for which there is room in it have been developed; and new, higher relations of production never appear before the material conditions of their existence have matured in the womb of the old society. Therefore, mankind always takes up only such problems as it can solve, since looking at the matter more closely we will always find that the problem itself arises only when the material conditions necessary for its solution already exist, or are at least in the process of formation.[11]

This passage clearly rules out any possibility of realizing socialism except in an advanced capitalist society. While it does not necessarily imply a doctrine of revolutionary patience, it does stand as a constant warning against revolutionary *putchism* and premature sallies.

In Marx's general statement of historical materialism we find no mention of class struggle—a concept which elsewhere figures so prominently in his writings. The following, therefore, is an attempt to clarify Marx's concepts of class, class struggle, and the relation between class and ideology.

Marx claimed no credit for the discovery of the existence of classes or the struggle between them. These facts had already been uncovered (he pointed out) by bourgeois historians (Guizot, Thierry) and economists (Ricardo).

> What I did that was new was to prove: (1) that the *existence of classes* is only bound up with *particular historical phases in the development of production*; (2) that the class struggle necessarily leads to the *dictatorship of the proletariat*; (3) that this dictatorship itself only constitutes the transition to the *abolition of all classes* and to a *classless society*.[12]

More will be said later about these extraordinary theses, but for now let us simply call attention to the dual origins of Marx's concept of class. The one is French and essentially political, based on the interpretation of the French Revolution by liberal historians of the Restoration. The second is British and essentially economic, derived from the analysis of emerging industrial capitalism provided by the classical political economists. The first examines the long historical development of the struggle between the Third Estate and the privileged orders; the second examines the conflict of economic interests among landed proprietors, industrial capitalists, and wage earners. It is obvious that speaking of both as class struggles misleadingly conflates two rather different historical phenomena. Doing so, however, allows Marx to infer that the emancipation of the proletariat (wage earners) is analogous to the emancipation of the bourgeoisie (Third Estate).

Now for Marx both the political and the economic were essential to his notion of class. That is, the economic struggle of one class against another at some point begins to take on a political character: the class strives to make its own interest the general interest, to impose its will on the society as a whole. A good example of this tendency may be found in Marx's letter to Bolte:

> . . . every movement in which the working class comes out as
> a class against the ruling classes and tries to coerce them by
> pressure from without is a political movement. For example,
> the attempt in a particular factory, even in a particular trade,
> to force a shorter working day, etc., is a purely economic move-
> ment. On the other hand, the movement to force through an
> eight hour law is a political movement.[13]

The transition from a purely economic to a political struggle is the characteristic of a true class. But Marx also recognized as a class groups such as the small-holding peasants in France. While having a "separate way of life, interests, and education" which put them in opposition to other classes, they were incapable of making the transition to the level of political organization and independent activity on a national scale.[14]

Marx often refers to class struggle as the "motor force" of history. In his view, the conflict between productive forces and social relations of production does and must manifest itself as a conflict between classes—a class which seeks to preserve the existing relations of production and a class which seeks to abolish them and put new ones in their place. This conflict also takes an ideological form in which rival systems of ideas represent the rival interests of the contending classes. But the relationship between ideology and class must not be interpreted in too mechanical a way.

> Just as little must one imagine that the democratic representatives are indeed all shopkeepers. According to their education and their individual position they may be as far apart as heaven and earth. What makes them representatives of the petty bourgeoisie is the fact that in their minds they do not get beyond the limits which the latter do not get beyond in life, that they are consequently driven, theoretically, to the same problems and solutions to which material interests and social position drive the latter practically. This is, in general, the relationship between the *political* and *literary* representatives of a class and the class they represent.[15]

This formulation—while considerably more sophisticated than the views commonly attributed to Marx—leaves unclear what it is that "drives" the ideologist to certain "problems and solutions." But it does allow Marx to take account of the possibility of cleavages—sometimes quite sharp—between the political and literary representatives of a class and the class they represent (for example, that between the parliamentary bourgeoisie and the extraparliamentary bourgeoisie in the months preceding Louis Bonaparte's coup).[16] It suggests, in short, that the relations between ideas and class is a logical one, an imputation of what the class-conscious individual ideally should think, not necessarily what individual members of that class do in fact think or even what that class as a whole thinks at any given time.

Applying this approach to the relationship between the socialist theorist and the proletariat, Marx's argument may be put as follows: The theorist becomes aware of the contradictions in society and proposes certain solutions. The statement of the problem and the solutions proposed reflect the stage of development of social contradictions, especially the stage of development of the class struggle. Hence Utopian Socialism was the typical expression of the formative and still immature stage of the proletarian movement.[17] But as capitalism develops and its contradictory character is more fully revealed, and as the proletariat grows in strength and numbers and forms a political party, the socialist theorists have only "to observe what is happening before their eyes and to make themselves its vehicle of expression."[18] Socialist theory, by correctly expressing the contradictions of material life and formulating the conditions for their resolution, reaches conclusions to which the proletariat is driven by material interests and social position.

Marx's theory of proletarian revolution can now be formulated in terms of historical materialism:

(1) The conflict between the productive forces and bourgeois relations of production must manifest itself as a conflict between classes (bourgeoisie and proletariat); these two levels of conflict must express themselves in terms of ideological conflict (liberalism and socialism).

(2) The abolition of bourgeois property relations is a necessary condition for the emancipation of the proletariat as a class.

(3) The antagonism between bourgeoisie and proletariat is the *final form* of class antagonism.

(4) Therefore, the emancipation of the proletariat is identical with the abolition of all classes and the creation of a classless society.

(5) Viewed in this light, socialism is merely the theoretical expression of the historical fact that the existence of classes has become historically obsolete.

(6) Socialism as theory thus corresponds to the practical needs of a class (the proletariat) inasmuch as the emancipation of that class coincides with the abolition of all classes.

In these formulations Marx has set aside the notion of the proletariat as emancipator of man and has put in its place the more empirical claim that proletarian emancipation is necessarily identical with the abolition of classes. This claim is absolutely crucial to the whole Marxian deduction.

Marx's Concept of the Revolutionary Proletariat, 1845-1883

Chapter 3

The mature Marx believed he had derived the revolutionary character of the proletariat strictly and empirically from historical materialism, without the addition of any a priori assumptions about human nature. This claim can be examined in terms of three distinct but related arguments. Section 1 of this chapter shows that Marx's concept of proletarian emancipation—though it purports to be strictly empirical—in fact contains a priori elements, that Marx defines his terms in such a way as to get the results he wants—results which could not be empirically derived. Section 2 shows that although Marx professes to derive his revolutionary theory strictly from a materialist analysis of historical conditions, in reality his judgments about actual revolutionary situations (those of 1848 and 1871) cannot be reconciled with historical materialism. Section 3 explores ambiguities implicit in Marx's universalist conception of the revolutionary mission of the proletariat.

THE THEORY OF PROLETARIAN EMANCIPATION

Marx's clearest and most succinct statement of the theory of proletarian emancipation is found in the *Poverty of Philosophy* (1847).

> An oppressed class is the vital condition for every society founded on the antagonism of classes. The emancipation of the oppressed class thus implies the creation of a new society. For the oppressed class to be able to emancipate itself it is necessary that the productive powers already acquired and the existing social relations should no longer be capable of existing side by side. Of all the instruments of production the greatest productive power is the revolutionary class itself. The organization of revolutionary elements as a class supposes the existence of all the productive forces which could be created in the bosom of the old society.
>
> Does this mean that after the fall of the old society [i.e., bourgeois society] there will be a new class domination culminating in a new political power? No.
>
> The condition for the emancipation of the working class is the abolition of every class, just as the condition for the emancipation of the Third Estate, of the bourgeois order, was the abolition of all estates and all orders. The working class in the course of its development will substitute for the old civil society an association which will exclude classes and their antagonism, and there will be no more political power properly so-called, since political power is precisely the official expression of antagonism in civil society.[1]

This passage puts forth two extremely important arguments. The first is that the process by which the proletariat will emancipate itself is analogous to that by which the bourgeoisie emancipated itself; the second is that the emancipation of the proletariat as a class requires the abolition of all classes. Both of these arguments are central to Marx's theory of proletarian emancipation.

For the professed analogy between bourgeois and proletarian emancipation to hold two conditions must be met: (1) the bourgeoisie must have been an oppressed class in feudal society and (2) the bourgeoisie must have occupied a position in the feudal mode of production analogous to that occupied by the proletariat in the capitalist mode of production. As to the first condition, Marx may be correct in saying that the bourgeoisie was an oppressed class under the feudal nobility before it formed itself into communes;[2] it is hardly plausible to characterize it as an oppressed class thereafter. Certainly, one finds it hard to summon up tears concerning the "oppression" of the French bourgeoisie in 1789. In fact, from medieval times to the nineteenth century the oppressed class in European society was surely the peasantry. This brings us to the second condition. The bourgeoisie did *not* occupy a position in the system of production analogous to that of the proletariat. However real and important the class antagonism between bourgeoisie and aristocracy may have been, it was essentially a conflict between two modes of exploiting labor, two elements of an exploiting class. To say that the vestiges of feudal society (guilds, corporations, feudal dues, obligations) constituted a serious obstacle to the development of the bourgeoisie may well be true, but one finds it hard to characterize this condition as oppression. The relation between the bourgeoisie and the proletariat, however, is one of absolute interdependence. It could not be said that the aristocracy directly exploited the bourgeoisie (or indirectly, for that matter), but it was quite plausible to argue that the bourgeoisie did indeed exploit the proletariat in the most direct and obvious manner. Moreover, whereas the proletariat constituted the basic producing class in the nineteenth century (or was coming to be so), the bourgeoisie had never occupied such a position under the *ancien régime*: rather it was the peasants who were the basic producers.

By this time, it should seem doubtful whether the analogy between the emancipation of the bourgeoisie and that of the proletariat still holds. One must inquire further as to what "emancipation" means in this context. Marx asserts that the "condition of the emancipation of the bourgeoisie is the abolition of all estates and all orders."[3] But the bourgeoisie was not identical with the Third Estate: peasants and *sans-culottes* constituted the overwhelming majority of the Third Estate. In any case, the abolition of orders and estates merely made "official" the actual division in French society between the rich and the poor, instead of clinging to the outworn medieval fictions.

If the analogy between proletarian emancipation and bourgeois emancipation does not apply, then Marx's attempts to deduce the necessity of proletarian revolution from his general theory of social change fail. Marx can no longer convincingly show us that the *necessity* of proletarian revolution follows from historical laws in general and the case of the bourgeois revolution in particular.[4]

What of Marx's claim that the condition for the emancipation of the proletariat as a class is the abolition of all classes? We must answer this question by posing two others. Why must the proletariat emancipate itself *as a class*? And why *must* this emancipation as a class imply the abolition of classes?

Presumably the proletariat must emancipate itself as a class because the bourgeoisie emancipated itself as a class. But did it? Many of those who were clearly members of the bourgeoisie before 1789 were de-classed by the so-called bourgeois emancipation of 1789. Conversely, many who were not bourgeois before 1789 became so after that year. What this "emancipation" really did was not to free a determinate group of people united by a common relation to the means of production, but to create a situation in which individuals (regardless of social origin) could, by dint of talent and energy, compete with others for wealth, office, and status. "Bourgeois emancipation" was thus, strictly speaking, an emancipation of individuals not of a class.

Why, then, must the proletariat emancipate itself *as a class*? No doubt Marx's answer would be that the proletariat is a hereditary caste and no individual proletarian can hope to free himself without freeing all. But this is a purely *contingent* argument—one which depends for its validity on an agreement about social facts and possibilities. If it could be shown that the characterization of the proletariat as a hereditary caste is false (or could be rendered false by social action), then the necessity of the emancipation of the proletariat as a class would be obviated. Indeed this was precisely the position taken by Lorenz von Stein. He maintained that as long as access to capital (material and mental) is open to all,

... this provides an opportunity for everyone to break through the traditional pattern of social classes and of the ensuing dependence. .... As long as this opportunity exists in the form of a rule also extending to the worker, no contradiction [between the social order and free personality] is apparent, and the social order is stable, no matter how great are the dependence and differences between the two classes.[5]

Sismondi proposed another solution to the problem of the proletariat. In his view there was a clear distinction to be drawn between the proletariat and the working class (a class which works for wages). What characterized the proletariat was not the mere fact of being wage earners; rather it was its subjection to the vicissitudes of the free market economy—its utter insecurity and powerlessness. If these conditions could be remedied —for example, by a minimum wage, guarantees of work, regulation of working conditions—then the proletariat (as distinct from the working class) would cease to exist.[6]

Now it is true that Marx would have questioned the political and economic feasibility of the proposals for social reform advanced above. But it was not principally on such grounds that he rejected them. Beneath his practical objections to Sismondi's reforms lies Marx's conviction that wage labor is inherently unfree and must be abolished. Beneath his practical objections to von Stein's position lies the conviction that the perpetuation of a class society—however "fair" in its own terms—violates the universal development of each individual, as formulated in the early writings. The necessity which identifies the emancipation of the proletariat with the abolition of classes is not an empirical but a moral one.

REVOLUTIONARY THEORY AND HISTORICAL REALITY, 1848-1871

Marx made judgments about two (there were only two) major revolutions during his lifetime: the continental upheavals of 1848-1850 and the Paris Commune of 1871. This discussion will show that his evaluation of these events was not in accord with historical materialism and suggest that this was so because

his revolutionary theory was ultimately founded upon certain
a priori assumptions derived from his early thought.

The Revolutions of 1848

It is obvious that Marx's theory of proletarian revolution was
applicable in 1848 only to England, inasmuch as it presupposes
an industrially developed society. Neither France nor Germany
in 1848 was "objectively" ripe for proletarian revolution.[7] Yet
throughout the 1840s Marx was completely convinced that proletarian revolution was on the immediate agenda of these three
countries—even if, in Germany, there would have to be a brief
period of bourgeois dominance, to be immediately followed by
proletarian revolution.[8] With regard to Germany, at least, Engels
spoke in the more authentic voice of historical materialism when
he said—with the benefit of hindsight—"the working class in
Germany is, in its social and political development, as far behind
that of England and France as the German bourgeoisie is behind
the bourgeoisie of those countries. Like master, like man."[9] (The
contrast between this view of the German proletariat and the
view expressed by Marx in 1843-1844 is, of course, striking.)

How are we to account for so fundamental a contradiction
in Marx's thought? How can the theory of historical materialism
be reconciled with the apparent revolutionary voluntarism of
Marx's pronouncements on France and Germany? Broadly
speaking, Marx attempted to overcome this by two distinct
theoretical models—what may be called the theory of the representative class and the theory of permanent revolution.

Marx modeled his theory of the representative class upon
what he believed to be the historical record of the French
bourgeoisie of 1789. This class—a minority of the population—
had succeeded in rallying the other nonruling classes of the
country to overthrow the *ancien régime*. From this reading
of the French Revolution Marx generalized as follows:

No class in civil society can play this [revolutionary] part
unless it can arouse in itself and in the masses, a moment
of enthusiasm in which it associates and mingles with
society at large, identifies itself with it, and is felt and

recognized as the general representative of this society.
Its aims and interests must genuinely be the aims and interests of society itself, of which it becomes in reality
the social head and heart. It is only in the name of
general interests that a particular class can claim general
supremacy.[10]

Engels puts the point even more tersely: ". . . one class of
society can and must be called upon to represent the whole
of the interests of a nation."[11] Now this doctrine implied
that the proletariat, though a minority of the population,
could and must represent the interests of the peasantry and
petty bourgeoisie. It should constitute itself as the vanguard
of a broadly based popular coalition. In such a situation—
that is, in France and Germany—Engels conceded that the rule
of the proletariat would be "indirect," inasmuch as it would
have to share power with the other classes, and even that the
eventual transition to direct proletarian rule might involve
another revolution—presumably against its former allies.[12]

The 1848 revolutions in France and in Germany did not
confirm this theory. To begin with, Marx conceded that in
the French Revolution of 1848 the "proletarian party" appeared as an "appendage of the petty bourgeois-democratic
party."[13] As for Germany, Engels recognized that the petty
bourgeois (and not the proletariat) had played the "decisive
part" in the events of 1848-1849.[14] Moreover, not only did
the peasants not allow themselves to be represented by the
proletariat (Marx insisted that the peasants were incapable of
self-representation as a class),[15] they constituted in both France
and Germany the mass base of counterrevolution. On the face
of it, one would have to conclude that the proletariat could
not (even if it had tried) represent the "interests of the nation"
simply because the other classes (peasants and petty bourgeois)
did not share the proletarian view of what those interests were.
Indeed this was the conclusion which Engels drew, writing from
the vantage point of the 1890s:

History has proven us, and all who thought like us, wrong. It
has made it clear that the state of economic development

on the continent at the time [1848] was not, by a long way,
ripe for the removal of capitalist production. . . . But it is just
this industrial revolution [which has occurred since 1848]
which has everywhere for the first time produced clarity in
the class relationships, which has removed a number of tran-
sitional forms handed down from the manufacturing period
and in Eastern Europe even from guild handicraft, and has
created a genuine bourgeoisie and a genuine large-scale industrial proletariat and pushed them into the foreground of
social development.[16]

In short, when the proletariat constitutes the majority of the
nation it represents the "interests of the nation" simply by
representing itself.

The second theoretical model, the theory of permanent
revolution, sees the proletarian revolution as a continuation of
the bourgeois revolution. The bourgeois revolutions of the
seventeenth (England) and eighteenth (France) centuries had
emancipated civil society from the State—that is, established
free competition. While these revolutions established the as-
cendancy of the "bourgeoisie,"[17] they also generated in their
course a proletarian opposition (the Levellers and Diggers in
England, the Enragés and Babouvists in France). Indeed Marx
went so far as to declare that the "proletariat" held power
in France in 1793.[18] However, this proletarian opposition
was doomed to defeat, since the material conditions had not
yet been created for the abolition of bourgeois rule.[19] Nevertheless, as each bourgeois revolution occurs under more advanced material conditions, the strength of the proletarian opposition grows proportionally and the more narrow becomes
the hiatus between the triumph of the bourgeoisie and the
triumph of the proletariat. In the case of Germany, for example,
Marx expected the triumph of the bourgeoisie to be a mere
prelude, to be followed immediately by a triumphant proletarian revolution.[20]

But this theory of the permanent (or continuous) revolution
could be turned to embarrassingly pessimistic conclusions. Writing in 1847, Marx noted that the German bourgeoisie was

so retarded in its development that it is beginning to
struggle with absolute monarchy and seeking to establish its political power at the moment when in all developed countries the bourgeoisie is already engaged
in the most violent struggles with the working class.
By contrast, the French bourgeoisie made its bid for
political power at a time when the proletariat did not
yet have interests separate from the bourgeoisie and
did not therefore form a class.[21]

In Germany, on the other hand, the bourgeoisie "finds itself
in a relation of antagonism to the proletariat before it has
yet constituted itself politically as a class. The struggle among
the subjects has broken out before even princes and nobles
have been got rid of."[22] This ingenious argument was intended
to show how easy it would be to plunge directly from bourgeois to proletarian revolution, but it could more plausibly
be used to show how not even a bourgeois revolution could
be carried through in Germany—which is what turned out to be
the case. The method of historical materialism appears once
more as a device for rationalizing conclusions reached much
earlier (1843-1844) and drawn from quite different premises.[23]
    The situation, however, is even more complicated. The events
of 1848-1850 in France had given Marx cause to reconsider his
entire analysis of the revolutionary process in that country. Instead of assuming (as he had previously done) that proletarian
revolution was the order of the day in France (and would coin-
cide with the English and German upheaval), Marx came to
recognize the peculiarities, or, if one prefers, the "uneven"
character of the French development.

In England industry rules; in France agriculture. In
England industry requires free trade; in France pro-
tection. . . . French industry does not dominate French
production; the French industrialists, therefore, do not
dominate the French bourgeoisie. In order to put through
their interest against the remaining factions of the bourgeoisie, they cannot, like the English, take the lead of the

movement and simultaneously push their class interest to
the fore: they must follow in the train of the revolution,
and serve interests which are opposed to the collective
interests of their class. . . . The manufacturer, therefore,
of necessity, became in France the most fanatical member
of the party of order. The reduction of profit by finance,
what is that compared with the abolition of profit by the
proletariat?[24]

Thus by a curious and ironic twist, the consistent application
of the method of historical materialism to France and Germany
leads *not* to a theory of proletarian revolution but to a theory
of bourgeois counterrevolution!

Even those for whom theoretical consistency is not the
highest value must be exasperated by now. The materialist
theory of history, under the bludgeoning strokes of the events
from 1848 to 1850, seems to have become the revolutionary
theory of impossible revolutions, a theory which does not guide
practice to victory but rationalizes defeat. But lest we too hast-
ily draw this gloomy conclusion, Marx adds that in fact no proletarian revolution—however industrially advanced the country—
can be successful except as a part of a general European event.
With the events of 1848-1850 in mind, he writes:

In France the worker does what normally would be
the task of the petty bourgeois, and the task of the
worker, who solves that? No one. It is not solved in
France; it is proclaimed in France. It is not solved any-
where within the national walls; the class war within
French society turns into a world war, in which the
nations confront one another. The solution begins only
at the moment when through the world war, the proletariat is pushed to the head of the people that dominates the world market, to the head of England. The
revolution, which finds here not its end but its organ-
izational beginning, is no short-lived revolution.[25]

Marx is thus able to retain his commitment to proletarian revolution on the economically backward continent only by aban-
doning the materialist method of history in favor of a faith in
military catastrophism.

Thus it may be concluded that Marx did not succeed in overcoming the contradictions between historical materialism and his revolutionary commitment. Historical materialism, rigorously applied, often led to anything but revolutionary optimism; revolutionary optimism (or, voluntarism) often flew in the face of historical materialism. If it is true to say that after 1845 Marx ceased to base history and politics on a doctrine of human nature, one cannot help thinking that his concept of the revolutionary proletariat remained rooted—however unconsciously—in the old mode of thought. In the last analysis, Marx continued to believe that the proletariat epitomized alienated man, man to whom his own nature had become a stranger, and man who had only one vital need—the need to become human once again. The theory of the representative class is, after all, only the old theory of the proletariat as the universal class which represents the *true* interests of all mankind. The theory of permanent revolution too is only an elaborate and shaky rationalization of the earlier vision of simultaneous communist revolution in England, France, and Germany—a vision derived from the doctrine of human alienation. In the last analysis, it was Marx's belief in the moral (and not in the merely historical) necessity of human liberation which informed his revolutionary theory.

The Paris Commune

The coup d'etat of Louis Bonaparte (December 1851) confronted Marx with a most puzzling and unexpected phenomenon. The revolution which had been unfolding in France since 1789—with all its interruptions and setbacks—had now seemingly "regressed" to an earlier and apparently suppressed stage in its development:

> In parliament the nation made its general will the law, that is, it made the law of the ruling class its general will. Before the executive power it renounces all will of its own and submits to the superior command of an alien will, to authority. The executive power, in contrast to the legislative power, expresses the heteronomy of a nation, in contrast to its autonomy. France therefore seems to have escaped the

despotism of a class only to *fall back* beneath the despotism
of an individual. . . .[26]

Marx looked for the explanation of this paradox in the per-
sistence of a "bureaucratic-military machine" inherited from
the *ancien régime* and enhanced by every regime since 1789.

> This executive power, with its enormous bureaucratic and
> military organization, with its ingenious state machinery,
> embracing wide strata, with a host of officials numbering
> half a million, besides an army of another half million,
> this appalling parasitic body, which enmeshes the body of
> French society like a net and chokes all its pores, sprang up
> in the days of absolute monarchy, with the decay of the
> feudal system which it helped to hasten. The seignorial
> privileges of the landowners and towns became transformed
> into so many attributes of the state power, the feudal dignitar-
> ies into paid officials and the motley pattern of conflicting
> medieval plenary powers into the regulated plan of a state
> authority whose work is divided and centralized as in a fac-
> tory. The first French Revolution, with its task of breaking
> all separate local, territorial, urban and provincial powers
> in order to create the civil unity of the nation, was bound
> to develop what the absolute monarchy had begun: cen-
> tralization, but at the same time the extent, the attributes
> and the agents of governmental power. Napoleon perfected
> this state machinery. The Legitimist Monarchy and the July
> Monarchy added nothing to it but a greater division of labor,
> growing in the same measure as the division of labor within
> bourgeois society creates new groups of interests, and, there-
> fore, new material for state administration.[27]

The triumph of this state apparatus, the executive power, in
the person of Louis Bonaparte was indeed a "regression" but
a regression which can only be understood in terms of the class
struggles in France from 1848 to 1851: "In its struggle against
the revolution, the parliamentary republic found itself compelled to strengthen, along with the repressive measures, the
resources and centralization of governmental power."[28] This

gave Bonaparte—a world-historical nullity—his chance to mas-
querade as a world-historical personage.

In considering Marx's analysis as presented thus far, one thing
is striking: his entire critique of the state power is essentially
liberal.[29] Instead of the members of society carrying on their
common activities freely (through voluntary association), these
activities have been absorbed by a parasitic state apparatus:
social functions have become state functions. The logical development of bourgeois society (ideally exemplified in America)
has been arrested in France by an anachronistic and parasitic
bureaucratic state machine. Moreover, this state machine is, as
a last resort, the great bulwark against revolution to which the
terrified bourgeoisie will turn to secure its class interests even
at the forfeit of its direct political rule. Consequently, before the
proletarian revolution can make any further progress in France,
this state machine must be smashed. This act, however, is not
itself the proletarian revolution, but merely a precondition for
its eventual triumph. This was made quite plain by Marx in his
letter to Kugelman, written during the Paris Commune, and
dated 12 April 1871:

> If you look at the last chapter of my *18th Brumaire*, you will
> find that I declare that the next attempt of the French Revolu-
> tion will no longer be as before, to transfer the bureaucratic-
> military machine from one hand to another, but to smash it, and
> this is the *preliminary condition for every people's revolution
> on the continent.* And *this* is what our heroic Party comrades in
> Paris are attempting. [30] [Italics mine]

Marx appears to be saying, then, that what is on the agenda in
France is a general popular revolution whose immediate aim
will be the radical democratization of French political life,
not proletarian communist revolution. The coming revolution
will be directed primarily against the state machine. This was
in fact what Marx foretold in the *Eighteenth Brumaire:*

> The revolution is thorough-going. It is still journey-
> ing through purgatory. It does its work methodically.

> By December 2, 1851, it had completed one half of its
> preparatory work; it is now completing the other half.
> First it perfects the parliamentary power, in order to be
> able to overthrow it. Now that it has attained this, it per-
> fects the *executive power,* reduces it to its purest expres-
> sion, isolates it, sets it up against itself as the *sole target*
> [italics mine], in order to concentrate all its forces of
> destruction against it. And when it has done this second
> half of its *preliminary work* [italics mine], Europe will
> leap from its seat and exultantly exclaim: "Well grubbed,
> old mole!"[31]

But if the bureaucratic state machine is so parasitic and anachronistic, why has it so long survived and even become su-
preme by the coup d'état of 2 December 1851? To be sure,
part of the answer lies in the direct material interest of the officials and officers in its perpetuation and expansion.[32] But
this could not be for Marx a sufficient explanation, as it would
imply that the state power was a truly independent power representing no particular social class. In spite of this illusion of
independence, of standing above classes, "Bonaparte represents
a class, and the most numerous class of French society at that,
the small-holding (*Parzellen*) peasants."[33] Marx's analysis of the
support for Bonapartism is exceedingly complex and sophisticated,
involving as it does the interweaving of economic, political,
social, and psychological factors. However, the details of this
analysis are not relevant here. What is essential is to understand
why (according to Marx) the small-holding peasants had to be
represented in such an *indirect* way.

> In so far as millions of families live under economic con-
> ditions of existence which separate their mode of life,
> their interests and their culture from those of other classes,
> and put them in hostile opposition to the latter, they form
> a class. In so far as there is merely a local interconnection
> among these small-holding peasants, and the identity of their
> interests begets no community, no material bond and no
> political organization among them, they do not form a class.
> They are consequently incapable of enforcing their class
> interest in their own name, whether through a parliament

or through a convention. They cannot represent themselves, they must be represented. Their representative must at the same time appear as their master, as an authority over them, as an unlimited governmental power that protects them against the other classes and sends them rain and sunshine from above. The political influence of the small-holding peasants, therefore, finds its final expression in the executive power subordinating society to itself.[34]

But precisely because Bonapartism rests on this mass base, Marx is optimistic about the impending doom of the now-triumphant executive power. For Bonaparte is caught in a desperate contradiction: as the representative of the small-holding peasants, he is bound to try to maintain them in their obsolete and miserable little plots against the irresistible march of capitalist society. Hence the schemes for "credit banks" and the like. But on the other hand, Bonaparte is also the guardian of the material interests of the bourgeoisie[35] and consequently is driven to promote the very forces which undermine and erode the social basis of his rule. The inevitable trend toward the concentration of property dooms the small-holding peasant to extinction and with him the Bonapartist regime. "With the progressive undermining of small-holding property, the state structure erected upon it collapses. The centralization of the state that modern society requires arises only on the ruins of the military-bureaucratic governmental machinery which was forged in opposition to feudalism."[36] Here the authentic voice of historical materialism is raised once again: the smashing of the state machinery is made *contingent* upon the capitalist erosion of small peasant property.

It is clear that Marx conceived the smashing of the state machinery inherited from the days of absolutism as a necessary but preparatory stage of the revolution in France and elsewhere on the Continent. Where this heritage does not exist (as in America and in England) no such "preliminary work" is required. It should also be clear that Marx viewed the Paris Commune of 1871 as the confirmation of his analysis of twenty years before in the *Eighteenth Brumaire*. In its constitution calling for the abolition of the standing army, election of all public officials by the Commune and subject to revocation at will, the payment of public officials a workingman's wage, the fusion of legislative and executive powers in the communal assembly, the disestablishment of the Church, and the returning of education to secular control, the Paris Commune "supplied the Republic with the basis of real democratic institutions."[37] As such the Commune may be said to be simply the most thoroughgoing expression of the popular revolutionary tradition dating from 1792.

Had Marx left it at this, the episode of the Commune would hardly occupy the controversial place it does in the subsequent history of Marxism. He could, in good conscience, have supported it as another heroic, albeit ill-fated, event in the long history of the French revolutionary movement. But as is well known he did not leave it at that, but went on to introduce a thesis which made his *Civil War in France* one of the most celebrated and influential tracts in the history of the socialist movement.

> Neither cheap government nor the "true republic" was its [the Commune's] ultimate aim. . . . Its secret was this. It was essentially a working class government, the *product* of the struggle of the producing against the appropriating class, the *political form* at last discovered under which to work out the *emancipation of labor.*[38] [Italics mine]

Even more specifically, we are told that

> . . . the Commune *intended* to abolish that class-property which makes the labor of the many the wealth of the few. It aimed at the expropriation of the expropriators. It wanted to make individual property a truth by transforming the means of production, land, and capital, now chiefly the means of enslaving and exploiting labor, into a mere instrument of free and associated labor.[39]

In short, the goal of the Commune was communism.[40]

In these passages, Marx is clearly attempting to integrate

the Paris Commune into his scheme of historical development. The Paris Commune is not to be seen as a merely political revolution but as essentially a social revolution. How well does this claim stand up to historical evidence?

With regard to the origins of the Commune, Edward Mason has demonstrated that it was the product of military defeat and national humiliation, and not the "product of the struggle of the producing against the appropriating class," as Marx would have it.[41] Mason also has shown that the communal insurrection of 18 March 1871 was most directly the result of the economic policy of Versailles (the law of the *maturities*, the collection of rents prorogued during the siege, eviction for nonpayment of current rents) which affected all classes (save the capitalists), but especially the petty bourgeoisie.[42]

Was the aim of the Commune socialist? Did it intend to abolish private property in the means of production? The social measures of the Commune were perhaps radical by the standards of the time, but could hardly be described as socialist. They included the abolition of night-work for bakers, the prohibition of employers from imposing fines on their workmen, and the permitting of workers to take over *abandoned* factories or workshops (as well as those deliberately closed by their owners), subject to compensation.[43] This latter measure appears to derive more from the practical economic problems of a besieged city than from any ideological conviction.[44]

It may be, as Engels later conceded, that "in the *Civil War in France* the unconscious tendencies of the Commune were put down to its credit as more or less conscious plans."[45] This, Engels goes on to say, was justified "under the circumstances."[46] Support for that interpretation may be found in the text of the *Civil War in France* itself.

> The greatest social measure of the Commune was its own working existence. Its special measures could but *betoken* the tendency of a government of the people by the people. . . . The political rule of the producer *cannot co-exist* with the perpetuation of his social slavery. The Commune was therefore to serve as a *lever* for uprooting the foundation upon which rests the existence of classes.[47]

Thus Marx's case does not depend upon showing that socialism
(or communism) was the conscious intent of the Communards,
but rather upon the logical incompatibility of genuine popular
rule and a social order in which the interests of capitalists pre-
dominate. Ineluctably and even at first unwittingly, a government of and by the people will be driven to erode the rights of
property in favor of the rights of labor. The ultimate and logical
consequence of this process (Marx believed) would be socialism.

All this ingenious argumentation, however, is thrown into
confusion by Marx's famous letter of 1881. The letter describes
the Commune in the following terms:

> Apart from the fact that this was merely the rising of a city
> under exceptional conditions, the majority of the Commune
> was by no means socialist, nor could it be. With a modicum
> of common sense, however, it could have achieved a com-
> promise with Versailles useful to the whole mass of the people—
> the only thing that could be reached at the time.[48]

Now it may be that Marx's attitude toward the Commune had
been influenced by the progressive turn in the Third Republic
after 1878.[49] Indeed it may have seemed to Marx that the real
gains in popular government may have been achieved not because of the Commune, but in spite of it. But whatever contingent factors may have influenced Marx's severe pronounce-
ment on the Commune in 1881, the judgment itself reflected
a return to the sobering perspectives of historical materialism.
As noted earlier, Marx had connected the progress of revolution
in France with the erosion of the economic basis of small peasant proprietorship. Socialist revolution, under the economic
conditions prevailing in 1871, was clearly at odds with the pre-
cepts of historical materialism. In 1871, as in 1848, France was
not ripe for socialist transformation. Not only did the Communards not "storm the heavens"; they lacked even "a modi-
cum of common sense."

Once again we are confronted with the contradiction between the requirements of an empirical theory (historical materialism) and the subrational roots of revolutionary commit-

ment. Marx's idealization of the Communards of 1871 springs from the same sources as his idealization of the Silesian weavers in 1844. Marx engrafted upon the hapless Communards the vision of human liberation evoked in his early writings.

> Human emancipation will only be complete when the real individual man has absorbed into himself the abstract citizen; when as an individual man in his every-day life, in his work, and in his relationships, he has become a species-being; and when he has recognized and organized his own powers (*forces propres*) as social powers so that he no longer separates this social power from himself as political power.[50]

In this passage from the *Jewish Question* is foreshadowed the mythical program of the Commune.

HUMANISM AND CLASS STRUGGLE

The fundamental ambiguity in Marx's thinking about the revolutionary proletariat (discussed in Chapter 1) was expressed in terms of a tension between the universalism of ends (human emancipation) and the particularity of means (the emancipation of a class). With the development of historical materialism, the ambiguity exploded into open contradiction. How, it must be asked, could the proletariat, engaged in a class struggle based on conflicting (opposed) material interests, be said to represent the true interests of its antagonist? Marx, it seems, would have to sacrifice either the universalist pretensions of the proletariat or its revolutionary mission. Characteristically, he sought to do both and ended by doing neither.

The tension between the proletariat as a universal class and as a particular class develops along several lines. First, the method of historical materialism logically *rules out* the universalism of the early writings. Second, Marx recoiled from the practical political consequences of the doctrine of universalism, but without renouncing the doctrine itself.

To understand how historical materialism logically precludes the universalism of the early writings, it must be remembered that the role of the theorist is to grasp and formulate the contradictions in society and to offer solutions derived from that analysis. In doing so, the theorist may or may not be aware of the correspondence between his analysis and the needs of a particular class, but as the contradictions in society develop in sharpness and intensity, the correspondence becomes fully apparent. Theory (implying a set of political, economic, and ethical beliefs) thus cannot escape its connection with the material interests of particular classes. Liberalism, in its various manifestations, corresponds to the needs and requirements of the bourgeoisie (its life situation); socialism, in the same way, corresponds to the needs and requirements of the proletariat (its life situation). Each system of belief promotes and justifies (however indirectly or unconsciously) the material interests of the respective classes. One seeks to preserve particular social relations of production; the other seeks to overthrow and replace them. Just as the material interests of the contending classes are opposed and irreconcilable, so too are the systems of belief which each advances. In this scheme of things there can be no question of communism being the "real," but somehow misunderstood, interest of the bourgeoisie any more than liberalism could be described as the "real," but misunderstood, interest of the proletariat.[51] Communism (or socialism) must therefore be seen as a class doctrine and not a doctrine of universal liberation.

Historical materialism provides no universal ethical standard for resolving the disputes between contending ideologies (belief systems). One may indeed be the wave of the future, the other doomed to obsolescence and extinction; but this can hardly be described as a universal ethical standard for measuring the one or the other. Each, in fact, is valid in its own terms and the resolution of their disputed claims to right is left to the ultimate arbiter: force and might. As Marx himself put it:

> The capitalist upholds his right as buyer when he tries to make the working day as long as possible, and if possible to make two working days out of one. On the other hand, the specific nature of the commodity that has been sold [to him] sets a limit upon the buyer's consumption of it, and the worker upholds his right as seller when he tries to

> restrict the working day to a normal length. Thus there is
> here an antinomy in which right conflicts with right and
> both are hallowed by the law of the exchange of commod-
> ities. Between two equal rights it is force that decides.[52]

For Marx, as for Hegel, "world history is the world court."[53]
God is, after all, on the side of the heaviest battalions.[54]

Marx looked upon the "universalism" of the early writings
as a potentially dangerous political liability. The pernicious
consequences of the universalist heritage were addressed by
Marx and Engels in the course of their polemic against the
"True Socialists," first in the *German Ideology* (1845-1846)
and then in the *Manifesto* (1847). The True Socialists, Marx
and Engels complained, sought to derive socialism from the
nature of man. Given that socialism was in conformity with
the true nature of man, its realization required only an appeal
to the good will and enlightenment of mankind in general. The
True Socialist prided himself on "representing . . . not the interests of the proletariat, but the interests of human nature,
of man in general, who belongs to no class, who has no reality,
who exists only in the misty realm of philosophical fantasy."[55]

This criticism of the True Socialists hardly constitutes a re-
pudiation of Marx's own early views: he had spoken of the
"emancipation of man" but only as a consequence of the emancipation of the proletariat. But it is obvious—and by 1845-1846
it had become grotesquely obvious to Marx—that to formulate
the theory of proletarian emancipation in terms of the emancipation of man (the shibboleth of Young-Hegelian philosophy)
was to invite precisely the kind of argument made by the True
Socialists. If indeed man was alienated, then all men were alienated and stood in need of liberation. These conclusions, once
drawn, implied that to identify with the struggle of one class,
indeed to condone class struggle at all, was narrow and one-
sided.

In the late 1870s the heresy once more reared its head, and
this time within the very precincts of the newly founded German Social-Democratic party. Against this tendency Marx and
Engels prepared a circular in 1879:

In the opinion of these gentlemen, then, the Social-Democratic
Party should *not* be a one-sided workers' party but an all-sided
party of "all men imbued with a true love of humanity."[56]

The point again is that the discussion of socialism in terms of
the interests of "man," "humanity," and "mankind" leads
to politically harmful consequences.

It would appear that Marx and Engels had good reasons—
both theoretical and practical—for dispensing with the universalist pretensions of their early writings. But did they do
so in fact? Engels's answer to this question was as paradoxical
as it was revealing. Reflecting in 1892 on his youthful work,
The Condition of the Working Class in 1844, he has this to say:

> It will hardly be necessary to point out that the general
> theoretical standpoint of this book—philosophical, eco-
> nomic, and political—does not exactly coincide with my
> standpoint of today. . . . Thus great stress is laid on the
> dictum that communism is not a mere party doctrine of
> the working-class, but a theory encompassing the emanci-
> pation of society at large, including the capitalist class,
> from its present narrow conditions. This is true enough in
> the abstract, but absolutely useless, and sometimes worse,
> in practice. So long as the wealthy classes not only do not
> feel the want of any emancipation, but strenuously oppose
> the self-emancipation of the working-class, so long the
> social revolution will have to be prepared and fought out
> by the working-class alone.[57]

While, on the one hand, this passage supports the position out-
lined earlier, it also provides evidence to show that Marx and
Engels continued to adhere to the universalist heritage of the
early writings. It is curious indeed to hear a Marxist say that
something may be true in theory but false in practice. But
even more curious is why he bothered to say it at all. Surely
historical materialism had explained well enough why the
capitalists do not and *could not* see their own emancipation
in the emancipation of the proletariat. Why, then, persist in
believing—even "in the abstract"—that the emancipation of

the proletariat is somehow also the emancipation of society as a whole? The answer lies in the fact that Marx and Engels never wholly renounced (indeed they continued to tacitly presuppose) the conclusions reached in the early writings, despite the fact that the logic of historical materialism rendered these conclusions untenable. The tension between the universalism of the proletarian mission and the particularity of its social base remained unresolved in Marxian theory. To abandon the universalist view of the proletarian mission would deprive Marxism of its implicit ethical basis; to make explicit the universalist premises would endanger the distinctively class character of the movement.

Economic
Theory
Chapter 4

Marx states that it is his aim in *Capital* to "lay bare the economic laws of motion of modern society. . . ."[1] In principle, this aim can be seen as an attempt to apply the general laws of historical materialism to the specific case of the capitalist mode of production. However, for the purposes of this discussion, the demonstrations offered in *Capital* are considered in their own terms, that is, independently of whether or not one accepts the general theory of historical materialism. The question is this: can the revolutionary character of the proletariat be inferred (without prior assumptions) from Marx's economic demonstration of the necessarily self-destructive nature of the capitalist mode of production? In other words, if we concede the validity of Marx's economic demonstration, does the revolutionary character of the proletariat follow logically from it?

The cornerstone of Marx's economic theory is the concept of exploitation. Exploitation occurs whenever one class (owners or controllers of the means of production and subsistence) is able

to *force* another class to work longer than is required to produce what it needs to consume, *as a condition* for obtaining
what it needs to consume. Thus exploitation involves an ex-
penditure of surplus labor (labor beyond what is necessary for
the subsistence of the producers), the product of that surplus
or *gratis* labor being appropriated by the owning, nonproducing
class. One class, which has an effective monopoly of the instruments of production and the means of subsistence, is *thereby* able to force another class, which has neither, to work for
the benefit of the former. Literally this means that one class, in
addition to producing its own scanty means of life, produces a
surplus by which the other class can live handsomely without
working. For example, the slave of antiquity—the property of
his master—was compelled to work for a time longer than was
needed to produce a quantity of goods equal to the cost of his
subsistence: he was, in short, forced to work part of each day for
gratis, or more exactly, for the benefit of his master. The medieval serf enjoyed the right to cultivate his "own" land (land nominally belonging to the lord) on condition that he perform
unpaid labor services on the lord's land for a specified number
of weekdays (often three). Though the legal relations which
govern the relationship between classes in each case (master-
slave, lord-serf) are different, they have in common these basic
features of exploitation.

Perhaps it is obvious that both slavery and serfdom are exploitative systems. But how can this be said of capitalism? True,
the means of production and subsistence are owned (mono-
polized) by one class (the capitalists), and the workers, being
without either, can obtain the goods necessary for the existence
of themselves and their families *only* by selling their labor-
power to the capitalist. But this, it is said, is not exploitation
because the worker is paid exactly what his labor-power is
worth: no more, no less. If this is so (and Marx agreed it was)
there could be no question of "unpaid" or *gratis* labor and
hence no question of exploitation. But for Marx it was equally
obvious that in this case there could be no question of profit
either. (Marx ruled out the notion that profit came from over-
charging consumers on the grounds that competition would

soon drive down the price to its natural level; and for similar
reasons he rejected the notion that the capitalist could derive
his profit from "underpaying" the worker.) Clearly, then,
there must be something radically wrong with the premises to
lead to such patently absurd conclusions.

Marx thought he had uncovered the fundamental error: it
consisted in failing to distinguish between labor-power (a commodity) and labor-time (the standard used to determine the
value of all commodities). Accepting with some modification
the view of the classical economists, Marx held that all commodities exchange at their value (that is, the amount of socially
necessary labor-time expended for their production). Labor-
power, being a commodity like others, sells at a price determined by the amount of socially necessary labor-time expended in the production of the commodities indispensable
to the existence of the worker and his family (wage goods).
But, according to Marx, there is no necessary connection between the price of labor-power (the value embodied in wages)
and the amount of value which the worker will produce. Put
another way, the laborer is paid according to what his labor-
power is worth, not according to the value he will produce
during the workday. The capitalist, therefore, can *compel* the
worker to work longer than he needs to work to produce a
value equivalent to the value embodied in his wages. Not only
can the capitalist do this: he *must* do this in order to make a
profit. Marx thus divides the workday into *necessary* time (that
required to produce a value equivalent to his wages paid by the
capitalist out of preexisting funds) and *surplus-time* (those
hours of work beyond the necessary ones, for which the worker
is *unpaid).* The value produced in this surplus-time is designated
as *surplus-value* and constitutes that portion of the product
which is, in effect, "appropriated" by the capitalist. Thus capitalism is not only an exploitative system (like slave society and
feudalism), but one in which this exploitation can be precisely
measured: the rate of exploitation is the rate of surplus value
and is expressed in the formula $\frac{S}{V}$ (surplus-time over variable
capital, that is, wages).

As Marx sees it, the dynamic of the capitalist mode of pro-

duction is the capitalist's "greed for surplus-value." Under
pain of extinction at the hands of his competitors, each capitalist must strive to increase the amount of surplus-value he
can extract from his workers. This can be accomplished in
two ways: (1) by prolonging the workday; or (2) by decreas-
ing the amount of necessary labor through increased productivity (mechanization, speed-up, and the like). In this way, the
capitalist is able to increase the *relative* surplus labor-time by
reducing the amount of time needed for the laborer to produce a value equivalent to his wages. Thus, fewer workers are
needed to produce the same volume of goods. The introduction of machinery, therefore, creates unemployment and the
formation of an "Industrial Reserve Army," which has the
effect of depressing the wages of those employed. Any tendency for wages to rise significantly beyond the "real value"
of labor-power is decisively checked.

But the introduction of machinery (technical innovation)
does not solve the capitalist's problems. Not only do other
capitalists soon overtake the innovator, but the compulsion
to innovate forces the capitalist to follow a self-defeating and
self-destructive course. The more he innovates, the larger the
ratio of constant to variable capital; but from constant capital
no surplus-value can be derived. Only human labor yields surplus-value (and hence profit), but it is exactly this quantity
which is declining relative to constant capital. The capitalist
is thus faced with a dilemma: if he fails to innovate he will
be swamped by his competitors; if he innovates he is inexora-
bly driven to kill the goose that lays the golden egg.[2]

Thus, in *Capital* Marx seems to assume that if he has shown
that capitalism must destroy itself, he has also shown that the
proletariat must be a revolutionary class. The exploited class
"naturally" must be the force which overthrows the capitalist
order and replaces it with socialism. The socialist revolution
and the collapse of capitalism are equally "inevitable."

But does all this really follow from Marx's economic theory?
At most, Marx's economic analysis shows that the appropriation
of surplus labor *by individuals* must cease and that *some form*
of social appropriation must take its place. But Marx's economic

analysis does not—and cannot—establish a necessary connection between social appropriation *as such* and the emancipation of the proletariat. Engels was well aware of this problem when he wrote: "The more productive forces it [the State] takes over as its property, the more it becomes the real collective body of all capitalists, the more citizens it exploits. The workers remain wage earners, proletarians. The capitalist relationship is not a-bolished; it is rather pushed to an extreme."[3] Basic to Marx's critique of capitalism and his conception of proletarian emancipation is the proposition that wage labor is in itself *unfree*, in itself slavery. While this theme appears occasionally in the later writings,[4] its clearest statement and fullest justification were worked out in the early works:

> . . . the worker becomes a slave of the object; first, in that he receives an *object of work*, i.e., receives *work*, and secondly, in that he receives *means of subsistence*. Thus the object enables him to exist, first as *worker* and secondly, as a *physical subject*. The culmination of this enslavement is that he can only maintain himself as a *physical subject* so far as he is a *worker*, and that it is only as a physical subject that he is a worker.[5]

In short, Marx's economic analysis provides the necessary but not the sufficient conditions for proletarian revolution. The case for the revolutionary proletariat *logically* presupposes assumptions which were not empirical but derived from Marx's a priori conception of human nature, from whose arbitrary premises he deduced the necessity of proletarian emancipation. But here lies the dilemma: while Marx continued to take for granted the conclusions of the early writings, he had in fact abandoned the method by which he had reached those conclusions. Once again the empirical method cannot sustain the conclusions and the conclusions themselves were reached by a method that was not empirical. By this unconscious sleight of hand, Marx sought to preserve his scientific pretensions and his revolutionary commitment—but ended by discrediting both.

Marx
and the
Labor Movment

| Chapter 5

In the introduction to this work attention was called to the
perennial gap between the revolutionary expectations of Marxian theory and the unrevolutionary performance of the proletariat. It was suggested that this "failure" was not the result of
changing historical conditions so much as it was the result of
defects inherent in the theory itself. Specifically, Marx's mature theory of the revolutionary proletariat, despite its apparently empirical form, remained rooted in the a priori assumptions of the early writings. This dependence engrafted upon
the scientific efforts of the later Marx a dogma inherited from
his philosophical past.

Another explanation of the gap between revolutionary theory
and proletarian practice has been advanced by George Lichtheim. As his explanation complements as well as contradicts
mine, it is necessary to examine his argument in close detail.

In his study of the evolution of Marxism, George Lichtheim
has advanced a profoundly original and influential thesis. He
writes:

We have seen how Marx and Engels anticipated the revolutionary upheaval of 1848 by the publication of the *Communist Manifesto* and how in 1871 Marx reacted to the
catastrophe of the Paris Commune with a qualified re-
statement of the revolutionary standpoint in his pamphlet
The Civil War in France. In between these two important
dates, the founding of the First International in 1864 had
quietly inaugurated the appearance on the scene of a new
political force: the modern labor movement, committed to
democratic socialism. Marx stood at the center of these currents; the streams of history converged in his person. In 1871
he enshrined the memory of the Commune in a pamphlet
whose grandiose rhetoric rang down the curtain on an epoch,
yet at the same time he managed to keep alive the heritage of
revolutionary utopianism. In the following year, he drove Bakunin's followers from the International and for good measure
affirmed his own belief in the possibility of a peaceful transition to socialism wherever democracy was far enough advanced.
Ever since then it has been possible for Social-Democrats and
Communists alike to appeal to his authority and for good
reason. The contradictions latent in his outlook were fused
into a doctrine which Janus-like confronted the beholder
whatever his angle of vision.[1]

Now Lichtheim may be correct in arguing that historically
the disappearance of the old revolutionary movement in
Europe after 1871 meant that in fact no successful popular
revolution would be possible in these democratic (or quasi-
democratic) industrial societies, that the labor and socialist
movements would in fact evolve along democratic and reformist lines, and therefore that the Marx of the 1840s and
of the *Civil War in France* was simply out of date. All this
may be historically true, but it does not follow that Marx
himself would have accepted such an analysis. To be sure,
Lichtheim claims to be using Marx's own historical method
to interpret Marxism. Consequently, he feels justified in dis-
tinguishing between what Marx said and did, on the one hand,
and the larger historical forces which shaped his thought and
activity—forces of which he may have been only dimly conscious. But Lichtheim actually tries to do more than lay bare

the unconscious logic of Marx's thought: he plainly means to say that Marx expressly and consciously held the views which Lichtheim thinks he should have held.

Another objection may be raised. Even conceding Lichtheim's argument that Marx turned his back on the old (Jacobin-Babouvist) revolutionary tradition, it does not follow that he repudiated revolution as such. Indeed, to say this would ignore the fact that he thought of the labor movement as a revolutionary force. This evaluation of the labor movement may have been mistaken, but it was Marx's evaluation nonetheless.

Thus far Licthheim's characterization of the Marx of the 1840s (and of 1871) as a "Jacobin" has been accepted. Such a characterization, however, is confusing and misleading. If Lichtheim wishes only to say that Marx's practical activity as a revolutionary in the 1840s was primarily (and, given the political conditions on the Continent, necessarily) in communist secret societies of Babouvist ancestry, and that such groups formed the extreme left wing of the "bourgeois revolution" (especially in Germany), then there is little to disagree with in this statement. But if Lichtheim means by this that Marx subscribed to Jacobin-Babouvist ideology, then he is surely mistaken. Marx's and Engel's participation in clandestine revolutionary organizations in this period was not the result of principle but of the impossibility of open political agitation on the Continent. In England, where the political conditions permitted open agitation by the working class, both Marx and Engels vigorously supported the Chartist movement. In any case, neither Marx's conception of the revolution, nor his conception of the ensuing revolutionary dictatorship, accorded very well with the Jacobin-Babouvist-Blanquist tradition. Marx saw the revolutionary initiative coming from the masses and not from a conspiratorial elite, and the revolutionary dictatorship as the dictatorship of a class, not a self-appointed, "enlightened" minority. However, Lichtheim is probably correct in saying that a full recognition of the extent of the differences between Marx and Blanqui did not come until the First International and even more until the smoke of the Commune had finally settled.[2]

From his misrepresentation of Marx as a Jacobin, Lichtheim goes on to set up a drastic antithesis between Marx the Jacobin and Marx the theorist of the labor movement. According to Lichtheim,

> Marx eventually came to adopt the view that working class activity provided the only yardstick by which the progress of socialism could be measured. In practice this meant that the character as well as the tempo of political action had to be regulated by the spontaneously formed aspirations and beliefs of authentic labor leaders—not by the pre-conceived notions of a self-appointed vanguard for the most part composed of intellectuals.[3]

It is clear that Marx thought that the progress of socialism must be measured by working-class activity, but that one could only measure this progress if one had in mind a goal toward which the working class was moving and which it must one day reach. For Marx the cardinal measures for the maturity (that is, progress) of the working-class movement were, first, the extent to which the movement recognized the need to conquer political power for itself and, second, the extent to which it recognized that the emancipation of labor required the social ownership of the means of production. It was in terms of these two criteria that Marx plotted the progress and maturation of the International. It would therefore be more correct to say that Marx saw these two criteria as the only yardstick for measuring the progress of working-class activity.

As to the claim that Marx came to realize that the character and tempo of political action had to be regulated by the "spontaneously formed aspirations and beliefs of authentic labor leaders," it is surely true that Marx was not about to argue that political action should be taken against these aspirations and beliefs. That would be tactically senseless. But it hardly follows that Marx had come to defer to the spontaneously formed aspirations and beliefs of "authentic" labor leaders. So far was this from being the case that Marx at the Hague Congress of the International (1872) let it be known that he thought it was "an honor more than the contrary not to be an English workers' leader, because the majority of them had sold themselves to the liberals."[4]

It may be taken for granted that Marx believed, or came to believe, that the "character and tempo" of political action should be regulated by authentic labor leaders, as opposed to rootless and sectarian intellectuals.[5] But the real issue is, *who* is an "authentic" representative of the working class? Lichtheim would like to contrast the sober, democratically socialist labor movement of the International with the drunken, romantically revolutionary sectarians of the Paris Commune. And yet Marx says of the Commune that its majority consisted of "workingmen, or acknowledged representatives of the working class."[6] And Engels, writing in 1874, asserted that the Commune was "without any doubt the child of the International intellectually, although the International did not lift a finger to produce it."[7] It is safe to say that the lukewarm support or, more typically, open aversion shown by English labor leaders toward the Commune was enough in Marx's eyes to make them "inauthentic."

Lichtheim is probably correct in seeing the Commune as the last gasp of the old revolutionary movement. Certainly this is what Engels thought when, in 1884, he described the Commune as "the grave of the old, specifically French, socialism"[8] —that is, Proudhonism and Blanquism. A somewhat similar view was expressed by Marx in a letter to Sorge in 1880.[9] On the other hand, in his letter just cited, Engels went on to add that the Commune was "at the same time the cradle of a new international communism for France." By this Engels meant (as his 1891 introduction to the *Civil War in France* makes clear) that the two, "specifically French," socialist sects—the Proudhonists and Blanquists—were compelled by circumstance to drop their favorite and time-honored slogans and to act to meet the practical needs and aspirations of the people. The Blanquists, the old advocates of revolutionary centralization and dictatorial state power, found themselves proposing a constitution for France in which local autonomy and direct popular rule were carried to their furthest point. By the same token, the Proudhonists, the advocates of "mutualism" and the foes of social ownership, found themselves the architects of the Commune's economic legislation, in which nothing was heard of Proudhon's schemes, but in which the expropriation of the workshops and factories of absentee owners was proclaimed.[10] The "sects" had, in short, become "authentic" representatives of the workers in spite of themselves. Whatever reservations Marx and Engels may have had in later years about the Commune, there is no record of their ever having questioned the fact that the Commune was an authentic expression of the aspirations and beliefs of the Paris working class. No doubt Lichtheim wishes they had, and thinks they ought to have, but in fact they did not.

Lichtheim goes on to say that in 1872 Marx "drove Bakunin's followers from the International and for good measure affirmed his own belief in the possibility of a peaceful transition to socialism wherever democracy was far enough advanced."[11] In mentioning these two events together (they both came at the Hague Congress) Lichtheim is trying to establish a logical connection between them. Since he, Marx, was on the point of becoming a democratic socialist, what could be more natural than to expel die-hard revolutionaries like Bakunin? This insinuation rests on the erroneous assumption that to be against Bakunin was to be against revolution and, conversely, to be for Bakunin was to be for revolution. In fact, the struggle between Marx and Bakunin had nothing to do with this question. Marx was certainly opposed to Bakunin's conception of communist revolution, based as it was upon the premise that the *lumpenproletariat, déclassé* intellectuals, and landless peasants— rather than the industrial working class—were the true "proletarians."[12]

Marx had explicitly ridiculed and rejected this view in the *Manifesto* and even earlier in relation to Weitling. For Marx to have opposed it again—and especially when its exponent was intriguing (as Marx thought) to wreck the International— should come as no surprise. On the other hand, Marx's actions in this case confirm Lichtheim's thesis that Marx wished the policy of the International to be shaped by authentic labor leaders and not by rootless, sectarian intellectuals such as Bakunin. Apart from the fact that he thought most of Bakunin's ideas to be hopeless nonsense, Marx had little trouble in showing that they were divisive and would wreck the International

if Bakunin's following managed to get its way. The removal of
the seat of the International from London to New York was
not, however, as is sometimes claimed, aimed at removing it
from the influence of the Bakuninists, but rather from that of
the Blanquists, who flooded London after the Commune and
who threatened to seize control of the General Council. Enter-
taining as they did the usual émigré fantasies about an imminent resurgence of revolution in France and seeing in the International an instrument for the hatching of their revolutionary
conspiracies, Marx was understandably anxious to keep the
International out of their hands.[13]

By 1872, then, Marx had taken up a centrist position, flanked
on one side by the anarchist followers of Bakunin and on the
other by the Blanquists. Both were "revolutionary," but Marx's
criticism of them was directed at their basic assumptions about
the nature, methods, and agents of revolution, not at their revolutionary stance as such. It is true that at the Hague Congress
of 1872 Marx gave a speech in which he speculated about the
possibility of a peaceful transition to socialism in England and
America.[14] A year before he had given an interview to a jour-
nalist from the *New York World* in which he had said much the
same thing:

> Combinations among workmen cannot be absolutely identical
> in detail in Newcastle and Barcelona, in London and Berlin.
> In England, for instance, the way to political power lies open
> to the working class. Insurrection would be madness where
> peaceful agitation would more swiftly and surely do the work.
> In France a hundred laws of repression and a moral antagonism
> between these classes seem to necessitate the violent solution
> of social war. The *choice* [italics mine] of that solution is the
> affair of the working class of that country.[15]

Nevertheless, when asked by the interviewer what he thought
of the chances of a peaceful solution in England, Marx replied:

> I am not so sanguine on that point as you are. The English mid-
> dle class has always shown itself willing enough to accept the ver-
> dict of the majority so long as it enjoyed the monopoly of the

voting power. But mark me, as soon as it finds itself outvoted on
what it considers vital questions we shall see here a new slave-
owner's war.[16]

Marx seems to be saying that in countries where the method of
peaceful agitation is possible, this method should be used, but
that whether or not it will be sufficient to effect social change
without violence depends entirely upon the reaction of the
bourgeoisie.

In effect, then, he did qualify his belief in the necessity
of violent revolution in the last years of his life. This qualifica-
tion, however, must be considered in the light of his work as a
whole. Marx had (at least since 1845) rested his case for the necessity of revolutionary transition to socialism on the historical
generalization that ruling classes have not given up their power
without a struggle. If in the 1870s he was willing to entertain
the possibility of a peaceful transition, it was a possibility which
would have to prove itself against the overwhelming weight of
historical experience. But, as the conclusion of the *New York
World* interview shows, there was little change in Marx's practical evaluation of the political situation in England. Moreover, one must keep in mind that apart from this little-known
interview, the only other source of Marx's "democratic socialism" is the Hague Address of 1872. One would expect to find
some further elaboration of this view, or at least some reference
to it, in the writings of Marx and Engels after 1872, but one
looks for it in vain. Could it be that the Hague Address, and
not the *Civil War in France*, represents a momentary departure
from the true Marx? Is it not possible that the views expressed
were motivated by the desire to counteract the image of revolutionary extremism which the International had acquired in the
wake of the Commune? Perhaps no definitive answer can be
given to this last question, but the one offered earlier seems to
provide a more plausible explanation, in the light of the cumu-
lative evidence, than Lichtheim's view that this isolated speech
should be taken as authority for a fundamental revision in
Marx's thought.

Having subjected Lichtheim's interpretation of Marx to a detailed criticism, I would like to make clear that I am not in disagreement with Lichtheim's argument *in so far as* it claims to lay bare the historical contradiction within Marxism. The core of this contradiction is surely that Marx mistakenly engrafted upon the modern labor movement the revolutionary characteristics which actually belonged to the more diffusely popular revolutionary movement reaching from 1789 to 1871. Less convincing, however, is Lichtheim's claim that Marx abandoned his belief in the revolutionary proletariat or that he saw any reason to do so. If the modern labor movement has turned out to be nonrevolutionary, it was contrary to Marx's expectations. In short, Lichtheim has attributed to Marx not only a consciousness of "unconscious" historical forces, but a hearty acceptance and endorsement of them. For this there is no firm support in the historical evidence.

Conclusion

Marx began with the problem of human alienation—the contradiction between man's true nature (essence) and the conditions of life in modern society (existence). By defining man as a free and universal producer, as a social being, Marx was able to locate the source of alienation in the economic relationships prevailing in bourgeois society. By extension, he was able to identify the producing class of bourgeois society (the proletariat) with man as such and the emancipation of that class with the emancipation of man.

Marx, after 1845, abandoned the a priori deductive method of the early writings, though not the conclusions he had reached by that method. While in later writings he sought to base his case for the revolutionary proletariat on strictly empirical grounds, this effort failed because the empirical arguments advanced were insufficient, by themselves, to justify Marx's conclusions regarding the revolutionary mission of the proletariat. Indeed, at each point these arguments logically presupposed the a priori assumptions of the early writings. Taking it one step

further, the method of historical materialism is logically incompatible with the universalist ethical premises of the early
writings. From this it can be concluded that the hidden tactic
of the Marxian enterprise lay in seeking to give empirical substance to conclusions reached by an essentially a priori method—
conclusions which could not be validated empirically and which
were even at odds with the empirical method he developed.
What Marx did, in effect, was to engraft upon the industrial
working class of early capitalism a set of goals and aspirations
which were derived not from an observation of its actual at-
titudes and behavior, but from the speculative conception of
man elaborated in the early writings.

If Marxism emerges from this study as fraught with paradox
and ambiguity, it must be pointed out that it is precisely from
these characteristics that it draws its momentous historical
appeal. On the one hand, Marxism presents itself as a system
of historical determinism in which normative beliefs (ideologies)
are merely more or less conscious rationalizations for preserv-
ing or changing the status quo and whose validation depends
solely on "success"; on the other hand, Marxism presents itself as a set of moral absolutes which provide the basis for a
radical indictment of bourgeois society and a vision of human
liberation. Marxism presents itself as a relentless critique of all
"humanitarianism" (the "universal brotherhood swindle") and
an affirmation of class struggle; it also claims to liberate *all*
men from servitude. Marxism shows why classes must have op-
posing interests and resolve them through force, while it rests
upon the proposition that the liberation of one class (the proletariat) means the liberation of society as a whole, including the
propertied class. Marxism presents itself as a rigorously scientific
pertied class. Marxism presents itself as a rigorously scientific
theory of society standing in need of no a priori assumptions;
however, its central doctrine—the revolutionary mission of the
proletariat—was derived in a priori fashion from a purely speculative doctrine of "human essence," which resists empirical veri-
fication. Lastly, Marxism is a system which purports to do away
with illusions and yet its very foundation rests upon the greatest
illusion of all—namely, that a class of men, stripped of all hu-

manity, must become the redeemers of mankind. If the proletariat has failed to carry out the mission Marx assigned to it, the fault lies not with the proletariat but with the mission itself.

The Concept
of the Proletariat
as a Social Class,
1825-1848

Appendix

This study has proceeded on the assumption that the conventional meaning of the word *proletariat* is sufficiently clear. As used by Marx and some of his contemporaries it designated the new class of factory workers created by the industrial revolution. Nevertheless, such a term as *proletariat* (or for that matter, *bourgeoisie*) is not a precise sociological concept and was even less so in Marx's time. Nor was Marx's use of the term consistent or exact. Apart from its inherent sociological obscurities, it carries with it a range of implicit and valuational meanings which defy precise definition. It may, therefore, be of some historical interest to examine the various efforts made by Marx and his immediate predecessors to formulate an idea of the proletariat as a social class.

Granier de Cassagnac in his *Histoire de la classe bourgeoise et de la classe ouvrière* (1838) sought to demonstrate that the working class originates from the proletariat, "which is a more general and widespread element."[1] This "primitive element" is a

mass, more or less considerable, of families and individuals form-
ing the lowest position, the lowest stratum, of society. Ordinarily these individuals and families live by the painful and daily
labor of their hands; the wages of the day before is all they have
for the morrow, and landed property, when they succeed in
obtaining it, is for them much less the rule than the excep-
tion. These men who are not landed proprietors, who never
have been, and whom one cannot venture to promise that they
ever will be; these poor men, obscure, without fortune ac-
cumulated and transmitted from father to son, and for whom
all the domestic traditions are reduced to gaining their daily
bread; these men are proletarians.[2]

Thus defined, the proletariat includes not only wage earners
but thieves, beggars, and prostitutes—the poor of all descrip-
tions.[3]

Pierre Leroux concurred with Granier de Cassagnac's definition of the proletariat, with one very significant reservation:
Leroux objected that it did not include the "workers of the
field."[4] This extension of the definition of the proletariat to
embrace the rural population is extremely interesting and
deserves close attention.

Leroux refers to Robespierre's distinction between those
whose income is sufficient for subsistence and those whose
income is not.[5] Leroux refines these categories a little further
by labeling as "proprietors" those whose income attains subsistence, as "capitalists" those whose income exceeds subsist-
tence, and as "proletarians" those whose income is below subsistence. Of course by "income" Leroux means income from
property. And by "property" he means land. Now by using the
above standard Leroux has no trouble in showing that of the
ten million classified as "proprietors" on the tax roll, fully
eight million own only a cabin or a cabin and a hectare of land.[6]
In other words, their property is not sufficient to enable them
to subsist without their working for wages. Of the slightly more
than two million remaining, who may correctly be classified as
proprietors, about 100,000 are "capitalists." These same capitalists own one-third of the land, the total product of which
amounted to 30 percent of the whole in 1826. By comparison,
the eight million referred to above—while constituting (with

their families) nearly 80 percent of the total population—produced only 20 percent of the agricultural goods. Moreover, less than half of the eight million owned any land at all and that portion constituted only one-third of the total land under cultivation. For Leroux, then, those peasants with some property, but not enough to subsist on, who must sell their labor for wages, are just as much proletarians as those who have no property at all. In both cases, they are dependent on income from wages in order to exist. With this criterion in mind, Leroux breaks down the French population into the following groups:

Property and Social Class in France, circa 1830

1.	4,000,000	beggars
2.	4,000,000	indigents
3.	4,000,000	wage earners (that is, with no property whatsoever, including houses)
4.	18,000,000	not having enough property for subsistence
5.	4,150,000	having income of 128 francs (but less than 491) from land
6.	750,000	having income of at least 491 francs
7.	230,000	21,000 livres and up

35,130,000

Taking the first four categories together, Leroux concludes that France has thirty million proletarians. And by "proletarians" he simply means anyone without property, or without enough property for subsistence.

The Saint-Simonians took a rather different view of the nature of class and of the proletariat in particular. For them the decisive division in society was between the "idlers" (*les oisifs*) and the "workers" (*les travailleurs*). The former consisted of owners of property who lived from the income derived from it without performing any socially useful work; the latter consisted of all those who performed socially useful work (for example, bankers, entrepreneurs, engineers, scientists,

artists, manual laborers, tenant-farmers, and so on) who did not
possess property, that is, "instruments of labor." To compli-
cate matters the Saint-Simonians later conceded that not all
property owners (*propriétaires*) were "idlers," that some were
"working-owners" (*travailleurs propriétaires*).[7] By implication,
then, it was not always the case that workers were nonowners.
Class conflict, as they understood it, was not primarily between employers and wage earners, but between the idlers
(variously called "capitalists" and "bourgeois") and workers
of all kinds.

> Today the entire mass of workers (*travailleurs*) is exploited
> by the men whose property they utilize.[8] The managers of
> industry too experience that exploitation in their relations
> with the owner (*propriétaire*) but to a far lesser degree, since
> in their turn they participate in the privileges of exploitation,
> which falls hardest on the wage-earning class (*classe ouvrière*),
> which constitutes the immense majority of the workers (*travail-
> leurs*).[9]

The Saint-Simonians go on to characterize the nature of this
exploitation in terms already familiar.

> The wage-earner (*ouvrier*) is not, like a slave, the direct property
> of his master; his condition, always temporary, is determined
> by a transaction between them. But is that transaction "free" on
> the part of the wage-earner? It is not, since he is compelled to
> accept it, reduced as he is to obtain the subsistence of each day
> from the labor of the previous day.[10]

But who are the proletarians? To answer this question it is
necessary to take note of what is perhaps the fundamental
premise of Saint-Simonian criticism of existing society—the
evil of the inheritance of property within the family. Indeed
for them this system of inheritance is the decisive factor in
the continuance of the exploitation of man by man: it is the
last and most entrenched privilege of birth.

> The moral dogma which declares that no man ought to be
> judged incapable by his birth has slowly sunk in and the polit-

ical constitutions of our day have expressly sanctioned it. It
seems therefore that today one would find between the various
classes a continual exchange of families and of the individuals
who compose them, and that by virtue of that circulation the
exploitation of man by man—if it continues at all—would be
fluid, at least with regard to the races upon whom it rests;
but the fact is that exchange has not occurred, and with a
few exceptions, the advantages proper to each social position are
transmitted by inheritance. The economists have taken care
to point out the other side of this fact—the inheritance of
poverty—when they recognize in society the existence of a
class of proletarians.[11]

For the Saint-Simonians, then, the proletarians are simply the
hereditary poor, the "poorest and most numerous class."[12] As
such, the class of proletarians includes wage earners (who are
always poor) but is by no means composed only of wage earners.

For Sismondi a proletarian is not merely someone without
property, nor is he identical with the class of wage earners.
Strictly speaking, proletarians are only those who live by *daily*
wages, that is, who are hired and paid by the day or week. They
have no settled occupation, no special skill such as that of the
artisan or journeyman.[13] They have complete "freedom" to
enter any employment and leave it as they please (or as their
employer pleases), but they have no security comparable to
that enjoyed by the traditional skilled workman who is not
hired by the day but for a long period, and who may hope one
day to become a master. Among the proletarians must also be
included agricultural day laborers, whose position compares un-
favorably with the *métayer* who has a yearly contract with the
landlord and can at least be sure of having enough to eat.[14]
The agricultural day laborer, however, must purchase (if he can)
his means of subsistence. Viewed in these terms, it is not sur-
prising that Sismondi declares Ireland to be the most proletar-
ianized country in Europe, nine-tenths of the population being
day laborers.[15] England is next with three-quarters of its in-
habitants being reduced to proletarian status.[16]
Putting the matter another way, while anyone whose income
is derived solely from wages is ultimately subject to the vicissitudes of the market (especially the demand for labor), only

proletarians, being the owners of unskilled and therefore easily dispensable labor, are *every day* subject to these vicissitudes. The impact of market variations on the proletarians is thus immediate, direct, and often catastrophic.

It is also important to stress that proletarians do not rise above the barest subsistence level. Their food is the commonest and most unwholesome, their clothing the coarsest, their lodgings the most unhealthy.[17] They in fact constitute the lowest stratum of society. Yet they are not identical with "the poor." Sismondi outlines this distinction between the proletarians and the poor when he writes:

> The Emperor Alexander was so astonished to see the common people in England clothed and shod like the *bourgeoisie* that he exclaimed: "Where are the poor? Are there no poor in this country?" However, the greater part of these people are forced to earn enough to buy these clothes, having no other property but the pay they receive on Saturday for the whole week. And more than one-tenth of them are on poor relief. There is more independence and happiness for the poor who walk barefoot or in wooden shoes and who have their thatched roof, a field, a garden and two cows, as the greater part of the peasants do on the continent.[18]

The basic difference, then, between the propertied poor and the proletarians is that while both live at a subsistence level, the former possesses the means of subsistence (food, clothing, lodging) himself, whereas the proletarian can only possess them by means of commodity-exchange (sale of labor, wages). He is therefore dependent on the will of others for his very existence. And if his labor is not wanted he has no way of getting food, clothing, and shelter.

With the work of Constantin Pecqueur, specifically his *Economie sociale* (1839), the term *proletariat* takes on a more distinctively modern meaning. According to Pecqueur, the most significant effect of the application of machines and steam power is the impetus it gives to "association." In order for individuals to use the machines they have to "associate their capital and labor, to combine their efforts, and to bring together large numbers (of workers) under the same roof."[19] The means of production thus takes on a necessarily *social* character. "The degree of concentration of workers will vary according to the kind of industry and the power of the total machines employed; but its influence will always be such that the isolation and privacy of individuals will be replaced by public life."[20] Industrial centralization, thus conceived, involves two parallel phenomena: (1) the disappearance of small workshops and small centers of industry;[21] (2) the formation of a class of machine workers, the proletariat. The proletariat consists of those who have no capital (either in the instruments of work or savings), who work and are paid by the day, and whose wages do not exceed what is necessary for bare subsistence.[22] But the novel feature of Pecqueur's concept of the proletariat lies in his exclusive identification of it with the new class of industrial workers. Thus proletarians are those workers engaged in essentially cooperative (social) labor under the same roof. They do not work and produce as individuals but as a collective unit.

If Pecqueur began, Marx and Engels established the tradition of associating the word *proletariat* with the new class of factory workers created by the industrial revolution. As Engels put the matter,

> The proletariat is that class in society which lives entirely from the sale of its labor and does not draw profit from any kind of capital; whose weal and woe, whose life and death, whose whole existence depends upon the demand for labor, hence on the changing state of business, on the vagaries of unbridled competition. The proletariat, or the class of proletarians, is in a word the working class of the nineteenth century.[23]

He goes on:

> There have always been poor and working classes; and the working classes have been mostly poor. But there have not always been workers and poor people living under conditions as they are today; in other words, there have not always been proletarians, any more than there has always been free unbridled competition. . . . The proletariat originated in the industrial revolution which took place in England in the last half of the last (eighteenth) century, and which has since been repeated in all the civilized countries of the world.[24]

Thus defined, the proletariat is not identical with the wage
earners as such, but only with those wage earners who are
the product of the new technology and industrial organization. Those urban poor who are not part of the new economic
order are demoted to the so-called *lumpenproletariat.*

Despite the admirable clarity of their definitions, Marx and
Engels were far from consistent in their use of the word *proletariat.* In particular, they seemed unable to decide whether
landless day laborers in the countryside were proletarians or
peasants, or indeed whether peasants were a class by themselves or a mere extension of the categories used to describe
urban class structure.[25] When used in the latter sense, the term
proletariat hearkened back to the views of Sismondi and Leroux, rather than to Pecqueur.

In summary, the word *proletariat* was used widely to desig-
nate the poor (who were often propertyless) and the propertyless (who were always poor)—in short, the lowest stratum of
society. While more commonly applied to an urban population—as with Granier de Cassagnac—the term was sometimes
applied to the rural poor as well—as with Leroux. It was Sismondi, however, who narrowed the use of the term to desig-
nate the class of day laborers, which distinguished proletarians
from the poor in general and from other, more traditional
and skilled workers (artisans). With Pecqueur and Marx, the
concept of the proletariat was further narrowed to include
only those wage earners who worked in large-scale industry
powered by machinery and whose labor was necessarily cooperative in character. Thus being poor, or propertyless, or
even a wage earner, did not make one a proletarian; it was these
attributes, combined with the social character of labor in the
modern factory, which constituted proletarian status.[26]

Notes

INTRODUCTION

1. I am indebted to Professor Heinz Lubasz for this provocative formulation. See his "Marx's Conception of the Revolutionary Proletariat," *Praxis*, 5: 1-2 (1969).

CHAPTER 1

1. Ludwig Feuerbach, *The Essence of Christianity*, trans. George Eliot (New York: Harper and Brothers, 1957), p. 1.
2. Ibid.
3. Ibid., p. 7.
4. Ibid., p. 26.
5. Ibid., p. 73.
6. Ibid., p. 181.
7. Ibid., p. 178.
8. Ibid., p. 270.
9. Ibid., pp. 274-75.
10. Karl Marx, *Critique of Hegel's Philosophy of Right*, trans. Joseph O'Malley (Cambridge, Mass.: Cambridge University Press, 1970), p. 40.
11. Ibid.

12. Karl Marx, *Contribution to the Critique of Hegel's Philosophy of Right. Introduction,* in *Karl Marx: Early Writings,* ed. and trans. T. B. Bottomore (London: C. A. Watts, 1963), p. 43.

13. Karl Marx, *On the Jewish Question,* in *Karl Marx: Early Writings,* p. 30.

14. Ibid., p. 26.

15. Ibid., p. 13.

16. Karl Marx, *Economic and Philosophical Manuscripts,* in *Karl Marx: Early Writings,* pp. 147-151.

17. Ibid., p. 166.

18. Ibid., p. 164.

19. Ibid., p. 162.

20. Ibid.

21. Ibid., p. 121.

22. Ibid., p. 122.

23. Ibid.

24. Ibid., p. 123.

25. Ibid., p. 122.

26. Ibid., pp. 124-25.

27. Ibid., p. 125.

28. Ibid., p. 126.

29. Ibid., p. 127.

30. Ibid., p. 130.

31. Ibid.

32. Ibid., p. 131.

33. Ibid. I have noted earlier a structural analogy between Feuerbach's theory of religious self-alienation and Marx's theory of economic self-alienation. Marx himself affirms this analogy in several places. The worker becomes poorer the more he produces, just as in religion man impoverishes himself the more he attributes to God (p. 122). With regard to the alienation of the worker from his work, Marx writes: "Just as in religion the spontaneous activity of human fantasy, of the human brain and heart, reacts independently as an alien activity of gods or devils upon the individual, so the activity of the worker is not his own spontaneous activity" (p. 125). Moreover, Marx's characterization of alienated labor as "self-sacrifice" and "mortification," as well as his characterization of political economy as the "science of asceticism," recalls Feuerbach's criticism of Christianity for its mortification of the flesh and sexual repression (pp. 125, 171-73). Marx also draws an analogy between the worker's relation to the capitalist and the laity's relation to the priest.

Every self-alienation of man from himself and from nature appears in the relation which he postulates between other men
and himself and nature. Thus religious self-alienation is necessarily exemplified in the relation between laity and priest, or,
since here it is a question of the spiritual world, between the
laity and the mediator. In the real world of practice, this self-
alienation can only be expressed in the real practical relation
of man to his fellow-men. This means through which alienated
labor occurs is itself a practical one (p. 130).

34. Ibid., p. 187.
35. Ibid., p. 132.
36. Karl Marx and Frederick Engels, *The Holy Family* (Moscow:
Foreign Languages Publishing House, 1962), pp. 152-53.
37. Marx, *Manuscripts*, pp. 132-33.
38. Marx and Engels, *Holy Family*, p. 51. Translation revised.
39. Ibid., p. 52.
40. Ibid. Translation revised.
41. Ibid.
42. Marx, *Contribution*, p. 58.
43. Ibid.
44. Marx and Engels, *Holy Family*, p. 52.
45. In his recent biography of Marx *(Karl Marx: His Life and Thought*,
New York: Harper and Row, 1973) David McLellan has claimed that such
interpretations "are mistaken—at least as attempts at total explanation"
(pp. 96-97). He argues that the concept of the revolutionary proletariat
did, in part, have an empirical basis. According to McLellan, Marx based
his view of the revolutionary role of the proletariat on a historical analogy
with the role of the bourgeoisie in the French Revolution. While it is true
that after 1845 he did develop a serious historical argument based on the
analogy between the revolutionary bourgeoisie and the revolutionary proletariat, he did not do so in 1843-1844. The citation from "A Contribution to the Critique of Hegel's Philosophy of Right," on which McLellan
bases his case, is merely a rhetorical flourish and should be interpreted as
neither historical nor an analogy.

McLellan's second line of argument holds that Marx's view of the role
of the proletariat was not unique even among the Young Hegelians, let
alone among the more politically advanced socialist intellectuals of Paris,
with whom he came into contact starting in late 1843. While it is true
that Marx's "discovery" of the proletariat can be directly attributed to
his association with socialist intellectuals in Paris, it cannot be said that

his views on the subject were identical with theirs. In fact it was against
these very intellectuals (for example, Cabet and Villegardelle) that Marx
hurled the epithet "crude communism" in the *Economic and Philosophical
Manuscripts*. These communist sects, who saw in the proletariat a revolutionary class, grounded their belief on philosophical premises (a vulgarized
version of eighteenth-century materialism) wholly alien to the philosophical anthropology of the young Marx.

46. Marx, *Manuscripts*, p. 156.
47. Ibid., pp. 175-76.
48. Ibid., p. 176.
49. Marx, *Contribution*, p. 49.
50. Ibid., p. 51.
51. Ibid., p. 49.
52. Ibid., p. 55. Also Karl Marx, *Critical Notes on the "King of Prussia
and Social Reform,"* in *Writings of the Young Marx on Philosophy and
Society*, trans. and ed. Lloyd D. Easton and Kurt H. Guddat (New York:
Doubleday, 1967), p. 353.
53. Marx, *King of Prussia*, p. 355.
54. Ibid., p. 352.
55. Marx, *Contribution*, p. 59.
56. Marx, *King of Prussia*, p. 353.
57. Marx, *Manuscripts*, p. 155.

CHAPTER 2

1. Karl Marx and Frederick Engels, *The German Ideology* (New York:
International Publishers, 1960), p. 15.
2. Ibid., pp. 13-18.
3. In the main, I have followed the position advanced by Louis
Althusser in *For Marx*, trans. Ben Brewster (New York: Pantheon Books,
1969), pp. 222-47.
4. Karl Marx, *Capital* (Moscow: Foreign Languages Publishing
House, 1962) 1:19.
5. Karl Marx, *A Contribution to the Critique of Political Economy*
(Chicago: Charles Kerr, 1904), p. 11.
6. Marx, *Capital*, 1:79.
7. Ibid.
8. Ibid., pp. 372-73.
9. Marx, *Critique of Political Economy*, p. 12.
10. Ibid.
11. Ibid., pp. 12-13.
12. Marx to Weydmeyer (5 March 1852), *Marx and Engels: Selected*

Correspondence (Moscow: Foreign Languages Publishing House, no date), p. 86.

13. Marx to Bolte (23 November 1871), *Selected Correspondence*, p. 328.

14. Karl Marx, *The Eighteenth Brumaire of Louis Bonaparte* (New York: International Publishers, 1967), p. 124.

15. Ibid., pp. 50-51.

16. Ibid., pp. 106-7.

17. Karl Marx, *Class Struggles in France* (New York: International Publishers, 1964), p. 125.

18. Karl Marx, *The Poverty of Philosophy* (Moscow: Foreign Languages Publishing House, no date), p. 120.

CHAPTER 3

1. Karl Marx, *The Poverty of Philosophy* (Moscow: Foreign Languages Publishing House, no date), p. 167.

2. Karl Marx and Frederick Engels, *Communist Manifesto* in *Marx and Engels: Selected Works* (Moscow: Foreign Languages Publishing House, 1962), 1: 35-36.

3. Marx, *Poverty*, p. 167.

4. There are other reasons for questioning Marx's contention that the transition from feudal to bourgeois society is analogous to the transition from bourgeois to communist society. The capitalist mode of production developed within, but more precisely, alongside of the feudal mode of production. At a certain point the latter allegedly put fetters upon the further development of the former. This (according to Marx) necessitated a social revolution, as a result of which bourgeois relations of production became dominant and feudal relations were entirely abolished. If, on the other hand, we consider the capitalist mode of production itself, we realize that bourgeoisie and proletariat do not represent coexisting but hostile modes of production (as the analogy would require) but rather mutually defining (even if antagonistic) elements within the same mode of production. For the analogy to hold it would have been necessary either that (a) the medieval serfs (and not the latter-day bourgeoisie) had carried out a social revolution, stripping away the fetters of feudal property relations, or that (b) the modern proletariat be the initiators and controllers of a mode of production not yet dominant but independent of, and coexisting with, the capitalist mode of production. Neither of these conditions has historically obtained. The cooperative movement cannot be considered as a serious example of the latter condition: the proletarian insofar as he becomes a member of the cooperative move-

ment ceases to be a proletarian in the Marxian sense, whereas within the "interstices" of feudal society the *bourgeois* is precisely defined by his relation to production.

5. Lorenz von Stein, *History of the Social Movement in France, 1789-1848*, trans. Kaethe Mengelberg (Totaws, N.J.: The Bedminster Press, 1964), p. 92.

6. Jean Charles Leonard Simonde de Sismondi, *Nouveaux principes d'économie politique*, 2 vols. (Genève: Edition Jeheber, 1951), II, p. 244.

7. See, for example, Karl Marx, *Capital* (Moscow: Foreign Languages Publishing House, 1962) 1:8-9.

8. Marx and Engels, *Manifesto*, p. 65.

9. Frederick Engels, *Revolution and Counterrevolution in Germany*, ed. Eleanor Marx Aveling (London: George Allen and Unwin, 1952), p. 8.

10. Karl Marx, *On the Jewish Question*, in *Karl Marx: Early Writings*, trans. T. B. Bottomore (London: C. A. Watts, 1963), pp. 55-56.

11. Engels, *Revolution and Counterrevolution*, p. 137.

12. Frederick Engels, *Principles of Communism*, in *The Communist Manifesto and the Principles of Communism*, ed. Leo Huberman and Paul Sweezy (New York: Monthly Review Press, 1964), p. 76.

13. Karl Marx, *The Eighteenth Brumaire of Louis Bonaparte* (New York: International Publishers, 1967), p. 42.

14. Engels, *Revolution and Counterrevolution*, p. 7.

15. Marx, *Eighteenth Brumaire*, p. 124.

16. Karl Marx, *Class Struggles in France* (New York: International Publishers, 1964), p. 15.

17. Marx modified this judgment in the case of England by admitting that the immediate result of the revolution in England was the *joint* rule of the bourgeoisie and the landed aristocracy. See *Marx and Engels on Britain* (Moscow: Foreign Languages Publishing House, 1962), pp. 348-49.

18. Karl Marx, *Moralizing Criticism and Critical Morality: A Polemic against Karl Heinzen*, in *Selected Essays by Karl Marx*, trans. H. J. Stenning (Freeport, N.Y.: Books for Libraries Press, 1968), p. 137.

19. Ibid.

20. Marx and Engels, *Manifesto*, p. 65.

21. Marx, *Moralizing Cirticism*, p. 159.

22. Ibid.

23. See Chapter 1 of this book, the section on The Theory of Revolution.

24. Marx, *Class Struggles*, p. 113.

25. Ibid., pp. 113-14.

26. Marx, *Eighteenth Brumaire*, p. 121.
27. Ibid., pp. 121-22.
28. Ibid.
29. Marx's analysis of the growth of the "state machine" in France exactly parallels that made by Tocqueville in his *The Old Regime and the French Revolution*, trans. Gilbert Stuart (New York: Doubleday, 1955).
30. Marx to Kugelman (12 April 1871), *Marx and Engels: Selected Correspondence* (Moscow: Foreign Languages Publishing House, no date), p. 318.
31. Marx, *Eighteenth Brumaire*, p. 121.
32. Ibid., p. 129.
33. Ibid., p. 123.
34. Ibid., p. 124.
35. Ibid., p. 131.
36. Ibid.
37. Karl Marx, *The Civil War in France*, in *Marx and Engels: Selected Works*, 2 vols. (Moscow: Foreign Languages Publishing House, 1962), 1: 522.
38. Ibid.
39. Ibid., p. 523.
40. Ibid.
41. Edward Mason, *The Paris Commune* (New York: Howard Fertig, 1967), p. 55.
42. Ibid., p. 155.
43. Marx, *Civil War*, p. 527.
44. Mason, *Paris Commune*, p. 24.
45. Engels to Bernstein (1 January 1884), *Selected Correspondence*, p. 440.
46. Ibid.
47. See George Licthheim, *Marxism: An Historical and Critical Study* (New York: Frederick Praeger, 1963), pp. 122-23.
48. Marx to Domela-Nieuwenhuis (22 February 1881), *Selected Correspondence*, p. 410.
49. Engels to Kantsky (14 October 1891), *Selected Correspondence:*

Did the French bourgeois republicans, who in 1871-1878 definitely vanquished the monarchy and the rule of the clergy and secured freedom of the press, of organization, and assembly to an extent unheard of in France before in non-revolutionary times, who introduced compulsory education and made instruction general . . . , did they act as a reactionary mass? (p. 514)

50. Marx, *Jewish Question,* p. 31.

51. To be sure, it may be said that farsighted members of the middle class may see the handwriting on the wall and be led to climb upon the proletarian bandwagon. But this is to be regarded as an act of prudence (or perhaps expediency) rather than an act of true conviction.

52. Karl Marx, *Capital* (Moscow: Foreign Languages Publishing House, 1962), 1: 234-35.

53. George Wilhelm Frederich Hegel, *The Philosophy of Right,* trans. T. M. Know (Oxford: The Clarendon Press, 1958), p. 297.

54. This point of view seems to be endorsed explicitly in the *Manifesto*: "The proletarian movement is the . . . movement of the immense majority" (p. 44). Here Marx and Engels do not hesitate to substitute a majoritarian for a universalist justificaiton of proletarian revolution. Yet while the universalist conception rests upon the authority of a doctrine of "human essence," the majoritarian conception rests precariously upon the authority of numbers.

55. Marx and Engels, *Manifesto,* p. 58.

56. Marx and Engels to A. Bebel, W. Liebnecht, W. Bracke, and others (17-18 September 1879), *Selected Correspondence,* p. 389.

57. Frederick Engels, *The Condition of the Working Class in England in 1844* (London: George Allen and Unwin, 1952), p. x.

CHAPTER 4

1. Karl Marx, *Capital* (Moscow: Foreign Languages Publishing House, 1962), 1: 10.

2. Marx recognized various counteracting forces which for a time check this remorseless logic. Among these he included the possibility of increasing productivity by means other than increasing constant capital and the possibility of cheapening the cost of capital goods. See *Capital,* 3: 327-34.

3. Frederick Engels, *Herr Eugen Dühring's Revolution in Science,* trans. Emile Burns (New York: International Publishers, 1939), p. 304.

4. Karl Marx, *Critique of the Gotha Program,* in *Marx and Engels: Selected Works* (Moscow: Foreign Languages Publishing House, 1962), 2: 19.

5. Karl Marx, *Economic and Philosophical Manuscripts,* in *Early Writings,* trans. T. B. Bottomore (London: C. A. Watts, 1963), p. 123.

CHAPTER 5

1. George Lichtheim, *Marxism: An Historical and Critical Study* (New York: Frederick Praeger, 1963), pp. 122-23.

2. Franz Mehring, *Karl Marx: His Life and Environment* (Ann Arbor: University of Michigan Press, 1962), p. 488.

3. Lichtheim, *Marxism*, p. 128.

4. Mehring, *Karl Marx*, p. 488.

5. Marx to Sorge (5 November 1880), in Karl Marx and Frederick Engels, *Selected Correspondence* (Moscow: Foreign Languages Publishing House, no date), p. 404.

6. Karl Marx, *The Civil War in France*, in *Marx and Engels: Selected Works* (Moscow: Foreign Languages Publishing House, 1958), 1: 519.

7. Engels to Sorge (12-17 September 1874) in Marx and Engels, *Selected Correspondence*, p. 350.

8. Engels to Bebel (29 October 1884) in Hal Draper, ed., *Marx and Engels: Writings on the Paris Commune* (New York: Monthly Review Press, 1971), p. 234.

9. Marx to Sorge (5 November 1880), in *Selected Correspondence*, p. 404.

10. Marx, *Civil War*, pp. 481-82.

11. Lichtheim, *Marxism*, p. 122.

12. Bakunin saw the issue between himself and Marx in the clearest and most uncompromising terms. He writes:

To me, however, the flower of the proletariat does not mean, as it does for Marxians, the upper layer, the most civilized and comfortably off in the working world, that layer of semi-bourgeois workers, which is precisely the class the Marxians want to use to constitute their fourth governing class . . . this upper layer of workers is unfortunately all too deeply penetrated with all the political and social prejudices and all the narrow aspirations and pretensions of the bourgeois. . . .

By the flower of the proletariat, I mean above all, that great mass, those millions of non-civilized, disinherited wretches and illiterates whom Messrs. Engels and Marx mean to subject to the paternal regime of a very strong government . . . .

By the flower of the proletariat I mean precisely that eternal "meat" for the governments, that great rabble of the people ordinarily designated by Messrs. Marx and Engels by the phrase at once picturesque and contemptuous of "lumpen proletariat," the "riff-raff," that rabble which being very nearly unpolluted by all bourgeois civilization carries in its heart, in its aspirations, in all the necessities and miseries of its collective condition, all the germs of the Socialism of the future,

and which alone is powerful enough today to inaugurate the
Social Revolution and bring it to triumph.

From *Patterns of Anarchy*, ed. Leonard Krimerman and Lewis Perry
(New York: Doubleday, 1966), p. 90.
13. Mehring, *Karl Marx*, p. 486.
14. *The First International*, ed. Hans Gerth (Madison: University
of Wisconsin Press, 1955), p. 236.
15. Karl Marx, "Two Neglected Interviews with Karl Marx,"
Science and Society 32 (Spring 1972), 1: 10.
16. Ibid., p. 16.

APPENDIX

1. Adolphe Granier de Cassagnac, *History of the Burgher Class and
the Working Class*, trans. Ben Green (Philadelphia: Claxton, Remsen,
and Haffelfinger, 1871), p. 84.
2. Ibid., p. 85.
3. Ibid.
4. Pierre Leroux, *De la Ploutocratie, ou du gouvernement des riches*
(Paris: Boussac, 1848), p. 23.
5. Ibid., p. 18.
6. Ibid., p. 23.
7. *"Le Globe,"* 22 March 1831, *Religion Saint-Simonienne*, (Paris,
1832?).
8. A somewhat more concrete analysis of the exploitation of the
travailleurs by the *propriétaires* is provided in *"Le Globe"* (7 and 21 March
1831). Here we find among the exploited *travailleurs* not only wage-
earners but also tenant-farmers, those who pay rent for lodgings, small
businessmen and peasants who pay extortionate interest on loans. The
conflict between the idlers and the workers is thus expressed in the
clearest terms: "The workers want a rise in wages and a lowering of
interest rates and rents of all kinds, whereas the idlers who live off
rent and interest and who pay wages want the opposite."
9. *Le Doctrine de Saint-Simon*, ed. C. Bouglé and E. Halévy (Paris:
M. Rivière, 1924), p. 239.
10. Ibid., p. 238.
11. Ibid., pp. 238-39.
12. Enfantin, for instance, speaks of "the poor class, the class most
numerous, that of the proletarians" (*L'organisateur*, 15 August 1830).
13. Jean Charles Leonard Simonde de Sismondi, *Etudes sur l'économie politique* (Paris: Trauttel et Wurtz, 1837-1838), 1: 35-36.
14. Ibid., p. 36.

15. Jean Charles Leonard Simonde de Sismondi, "Landed Property," *Political Economy and the Philosophy of Government* (New York: Augustus M. Kelley Publishers, 1966), p. 171.

16. Ibid.

17. Jean Charles Leonard Simonde de Sismondi, *Du sort des ouvriers dans la manufacture* (Paris: Moquet, 1830s), pp. 3-4.

18. Jean Charles Leonard Simonde de Sismondi, *Nouveaux Principes d'économie politique* (Genève: Edition Jeheber, 1951), 1: 216.

19. Constantin Pecqueur, *Economie sociale* (Paris: Desessart, 1839), 1: 55.

20. Ibid., p. 63.

21. Ibid., pp. 262-63.

22. Ibid., pp. 273, 408-9.

23. Frederick Engels, *Principles of Communism*, in *The Communist Manifesto and the Principles of Communism*, ed. Leo Huberman and Paul Sweezy (New York: Monthly Review Press, 1964), p. 67.

24. Ibid.

25. To take one instance, Engels devotes an entire chapter to a discussion of the "agricultural proletariat" in *The Condition of the Working Class in England in 1844* (London: George Allen and Unwin, 1952), pp. 261-75.

26. For a similar survey of the subject of this appendix, see Goetz Briefs, *The Proletariat* (New York: Charles Scribner and Sons, 1937), chap. 2.

Bibliography

PRIMARY SOURCES

Books

Bouglé, C., and Halévy, E., eds. *Doctrine de Saint-Simon. Exposition,* première année, 1829. Nouv. ed. Paris: M. Rivière, 1924.

Dommanget, Maurice, ed. *Les Idées politiques et sociales d'Auguste Blanqui.* Paris: M. Rivière, 1957.

——. *Pages choisis de Babeuf.* Recueilles, commentées, annotées avec une introduction et une bibliographie critique par M. Dommanget. Paris: Colin, 1935.

Draper, Hal, ed. *Karl Marx and Frederick Engels: Writings on the Paris Commune.* New York: Monthly Review Press, 1971.

Engels, Frederick. *The Condition of the Working Class in England in 1844.* London: George Allen and Unwin, 1952 (reprint).

——. *Herr Eugen Duhring's Revolution in Science.* Translated by Emile Burns. New York: International Publishers, 1939.

——. *Revolution and Counterrevolution in Germany.* Edited by Eleanor Marx Aveling. (Authorship erroneously attributed to Marx.) London: George Allen and Unwin, 1952.

Feuerbach, Ludwig. *The Essence of Christianity.* Translated by George Eliot. New York: Harper and Brothers, 1957.

——. *The Fiery Brook: Selected Writings of Ludwig Feuerbach.* Translated with an introduction by Zawar Hanfi. New York: Anchor Books, 1972.

Fourier, Charles. *Le Nouveau Monde Industriel et Sociétaire. Oeuvres Complètes,* tome 6. Paris: Edition Anthropos, 1966.

Granier de Cassagnac, Adolphe. *History of the Burgher Class and the Working Class.* Translated by Ben Green. Philadelphia: Claxton, Remsen, and Haffelfinger, 1871.

Hall, Charles. *The Effects of Civilization on the People of Europe.* New York: Augustus M. Kelley Publishers, 1967.

Hegel, G. W. F. *The Phenomenology of Mind.* Translated by J. B. Baillie. London: George Allen and Unwin, 1961.

——. *The Philosophy of History.* Translated by J. Sibree. London-New York: The Colonial Press, 1900.

——. *The Philosophy of Right.* Translated by T. M. Know. Oxford: The Clarendon Press, 1958.

Hodgskin, Thomas. *Labour Defended against the Claims of Capital.* London: Hammersmith Bookshop, 1964.

Leroux, Pierre. *De la Ploutocratie, ou du gouvernement des riches.* Paris: Boussac, 1848.

Marx, Karl. *Capital,* 3 vols. Moscow: Foreign Languages Publishing House, 1962.

——. *Class Struggles in France.* New York: International Publishers, 1964.

——. *A Contribution to the Critique of Political Economy.* Chicago: Charles Kerr, 1904.

——. *Critique of Hegel's Philosophy of Right.* Translated by Joseph O'Malley. Cambridge: Cambridge University Press, 1970.

——. *Die Frühschriften.* Herausgegeben von Siegfried Landshut. Stuttgart: Alfred Kröner Verlag, 1964.

——. *The Eighteenth Brumaire of Louis Bonaparte.* New York: International Publishers, 1967.

——. *The Grundrisse.* Translated with an introduction by Martin Nicholaus. New York: Vintage Books, 1973.

——. *Karl Marx: Early Writings.* Translated by T. B. Bottomore. London: C. A. Watts, 1963.

——. *The Poverty of Philosophy.* Moscow: Foreign Languages Publishing House, no date.

——. *Pre-Capitalist Economic Formations.* Edited and introduced by Eric Hobsbawm. New York: International Publishers, 1967.

——. *Selected Essays by Karl Marx.* Translated by H. J. Stenning. Freeport, N.Y.: Books for Libraries Press, 1968.

——. *Writings of the Young Marx on Philosophy and Society.* Edited and translated by Lloyd Easton and Kurt H. Guddat. New York: Doubleday, 1967.

Marx, Karl, and Engels, Frederick. *The Communist Manifesto and the Principles of Communism.* Edited by Leo Huberman and Paul Sweezy. New York: Monthly Review Press, 1964.

——. *The German Ideology.* New York: International Publishers, 1960.

——. *The Holy Family.* Moscow: Foreign Languages Publishing House, 1962.

——. *Letters to Americans, 1848-1895.* New York: International Publishers, 1963.

——. *Marx and Engels on Britain.* Moscow: Foreign Languages Publishing House, 1962.

——. *Marx and Engels on Religion.* New York: Schocken Books, 1964.

——. *Selected Correspondence.* Moscow: Foreign Languages Publishing House, no date.

——. *Selected Works,* 2 vols. Moscow: Foreign Languages Publishing House, 1962.

——. *Werke.* Berlin: Dietz Verlag, 1956-1958.

Pecqueur, Constantin. *Des améliorations matérielles dans leurs rapports avec la liberté.* Paris: C. Gosselin, 1841.

——. *Economie sociale. Des intérêts du commerce, de l'industrie et de l'agriculture, et de la civilization en général, sous l'influence des applications de la vapeur. Machines fixes. Chemins de fer. Bateaux à vapeur, etc.* Paris: Desessart, 1839.

Ricardo, David. *The Principles of Political Economy.* London: J. M. Dent and Sons, 1962.

Saint-Simon, Comte Henri de. *Oeuvres.* Paris: Edition Anthropos, 1965.

Simonde de Sismondi, Jean Charles Leonard. *Etudes sur l'économie politique.* Paris: Trauttel et Wurt, 1837-1838.

——. *Nouveaux principes d'économie politique.* 2 vols. Genève: Edition Jeheber, 1951.

——. *Political Economy and the Philosophy of Government.* Translator unknown. New York: Augustus M. Kelley Publishers, 1966.

——. *Revue Encyclopédique* (Review of William Thompson's "Inquiry"), 22.

——. *Du sort des ouvriers dans la manufacture.* Paris: Moquet, 1830s.

Smith, Adam. *An Inquiry into the Nature and Causes of the Wealth of Nations.* Edited by Edwin Cannan. New York: Modern Library, 1937.

Stein, Lorenz von. *The History of the Social Movement in France, 1789-*

1850. Introduced, edited, and translated by Kaethe Mengelberg. Totaws, N.J.: The Bedminster Press, 1964.

Thompson, William. *An Inquiry into the Principles of the Distribution of Wealth Most Conducive to Human Happiness.* New York: Augustus M. Kelley Publishers, 1963.

———. *Labour Rewarded.* New York: Augustus M. Kelley Publishers, 1969.

Periodicals

L'Organisateur. Paris: 1829-1831.

Le Producteur: Journal philosophique de l'industrie, des sciences et beaux arts. Paris: 1825-1826.

Religion Saint-Simonienne. Extracts from *"Le Globe."* Paris: 1832.

Articles

Marx, Karl. "Two Neglected Interviews with Karl Marx," *Science and Society,* vol. 36, no. 1, spring 1972.

SECONDARY SOURCES

Books

Acton, H. B. *The Illusion of the Epoch.* London: Cohen and West, 1962.

Althusser, Louis. *For Marx.* Translated by Ben Brewster. New York: Pantheon Books, 1969.

Avineri, Shlomo. *The Political and Social Thought of Karl Marx.* Cambridge: Cambridge University Press, 1969.

Blumenberg, Werner. *A Portrait of Marx.* Translated by Howard Scott. New York: Herder and Herder, 1972.

Braunthal, Julius. *History of the International* 1. New York: Frederick Praeger, 1967.

Briefs, Goetz. *The Proletariat.* New York: Charles Scribner and Sons, 1937.

Briggs, Asa. *Chartist Studies.* London: Macmillan, 1965.

Charléty, Sebastien. *Historie du Saint-Simonisme.* Paris: P. Hartmann, 1931.

Chevalier, Louis. *Classes laborieuses et classes dangereuses à Paris pendant la première moitié du XIX siècle.* Paris: Plon, 1958.

Cole, G. D. H. *A History of Socialist Thought.* 6 vols. New York: St. Martin's Press, 1965.

Dahrendorf, Ralf. *Class and Class Conflict in Industrial Society.* Stanford, Calif.: Stanford University Press, 1959.

Dolléans, E. *Histoire du mouvement ouvrier* 1. Paris: Colin, 1957.

Droz, Jacques. *Europe Between Revolutions.* New York: Harper and Row 1968.

Durkheim, Emile. *Socialism.* Edited by Alvin W. Gouldner. New York: Collier Books, 1962.

Evans, David Owen. *Social Romanticism in France, 1830-1848.* Oxford: Clarendon Press, 1951.

Feuer, Lewis. *Marx and the Intellectuals.* New York: Doubleday, 1969.

Gay, Peter. *The Dilemma of Democratic Socialism.* New York: Collier Books, 1962.

Gerth, Hans, ed. *The First International.* Madison: University of Wisconsin Press, 1955.

Gide, Charles, and Rist, Charles. *A History of Economic Doctrines.* Translated by R. Richards. New York: D. C. Heath, 1913.

Halévy, Elie. *The Era of Tyrannies.* Translated by R. K. Webb. New York: Doubleday, 1965.

Hamerow, T. *Restoration, Revolution, and Reaction: Economics and Politics in Germany 1815-1871.* Princeton: Princeton University Press, 1958.

Hippolite, Jean. *Studies in Hegel and Marx.* Translated by John O'Neill. New York: Basic Books, 1969.

Hobsbawm, Eric. *The Age of Revolution: Europe 1789-1848.* London: Weidenfeld and Nicolson, 1962.

——. *Industry and Empire. An Economic History of Britain Since 1750.* London: Weidenfeld and Nicolson, 1968.

——. *Labouring Men.* New York: Basic Books, 1964.

Hook, Sidney. *From Hegel to Marx.* Ann Arbor: University of Michigan Press, 1962.

Jellinek, Frank. *The Paris Commune.* New York: Grosset and Dunlap, 1965.

Juczynski, Jurgen. *The Rise of the Working Class.* Translated by C. T. A. Ray. London: Weidenfeld and Nicolson, 1967.

Krimerman, Leonard, and Perry, Lewis, eds. *Patterns of Anarchy.* New York: Doubleday, 1966.

Labrousse, Camille Ernest. *Le Movement ouvrier et les idées sociales 3.* Paris: Centre du documentation universitaire, 1948.

Leff, Gordon. *The Tyranny of Concepts: A Critique of Marxism.* University, Ala: University of Alabama Press, 1969.

Lichtheim, George. *The Concept of Ideology.* New York: Random House, 1967.

——. *From Marx to Hegel.* New York: Herder and Herder, 1971.

——. *Marxism: An Historical and Critical Study.* New York: Frederick Praeger, 1963.

——. *Marxism in France.* New York: Columbia University Press, 1966.

——. *The Origins of Socialism.* New York: Frederick Praeger, 1969.

——. *A Short History of Socialism.* New York: Frederick Praeger, 1970.

Loubère, Leo A. *Louis Blanc.* Evanston, Ill.: Northwestern University Press, 1961.

Löwith, Karl. *From Hegel to Nietzsche.* New York: Doubleday, 1967.

Lukàcs, Georg. *History and Class Consciousness.* Translated by Rodney Livingstone. Cambridge, Mass.: MIT Press, 1971.

MacIntyre, Alisdair. *Marxism and Christianity.* New York: Schocken Books, 1968.

McLellan, David. *Karl Marx: His Life and Thought.* New York: Harper and Row, 1973.

Manuel, Frank. *The New World of Henri Saint-Simon.* Notre Dame, Ind.: University of Notre Dame Press, 1963.

——. *The Prophets of Paris.* New York: Harper and Row, 1965.

Marcuse, Herbert. *One Dimensional Man.* Boston: Beacon Press, 1964.

——. *Reason and Revolution.* New York: The Humanities Press, 1963.

Mason, Edward. *The Paris Commune.* New York: Howard Fertig, 1967.

Mayer, Gustav. *Frederick Engels.* New York: Howard Fertig, 1969.

Mehring, Franz. *Karl Marx: His Life and Environment.* Translated by Edward Fitzgerald. Ann Arbor: University of Michigan Press, 1962.

Mézaros, Istvan, ed. *History and Class Consciousness.* London: Routledge and Kegan Paul, 1971.

Ossowski, Stanislas. *Class Structure in the Social Consciousness.* Translated by Sheila Patterson. New York: The Free Press of Glencoe, 1963.

Plekhanov, George. *Utopian Socialism in the Nineteenth Century.* Moscow: Foreign Languages Publishing House, no date.

Riasanovsky, Nicholas. *The Teachings of Charles Fourier.* Berkeley: University of California Press, 1969.

Robertson, Priscilla. *The Revolutions of 1848.* New York: Harper and Row, 1960.

Roll, Eric. *A History of Economic Thought.* New York: John Wiley and Sons, 1964.

Rudé, George. *The Crowd in History.* New York: John Wiley and Sons, 1964.

Schlesinger, Rudolf. *Marx, His Time and Ours.* London: Routledge, 1950.

Schumpeter, Joseph. *Capitalism, Socialism and Democracy.* New York: Harper and Row, 1962.

Sée, Henri. *Le notion de classes sociales chez les Saint-Simoniens.* Paris: M. Rivière, 1920s.

Soboul, Albert. *The Parisian Sans-Culottes and the French Revolution.* Oxford: The Clarendon Press, 1964.
Sombart, Werner. *Socialism and the Social Movement.* Translated by M. Epstein. New York: Augustus M. Kelley, Publishers, 1965.
Spitzer, Alan Barrie. *The Revolutionary Theories of Louis Auguste Blanqui.* New York: Columbia University Press, 1957.
Sweezy, Paul. *The Theory of Capitalist Development.* London: Dennis Dobson, 1946.
Talmon, J. L. *The Origins of Totalitarian Democracy.* New York: Frederick Praeger, 1960.
———. *Political Messianism: The Romantic Phase.* New York: Frederick Praeger, 1960.
Thompson, Edward P. *The Making of the English Working Class.* New York: Vintage Books, Random House, 1963.
Tocqueville, Alexis de. *Recollections.* Translated by George Lawrence. New York: Doubleday, 1970.
Venable, Vernon. *Human Nature: The Marxian View.* New York: World Publishing, 1966.
Williams, Raymond. *Culture and Society.* New York: Harper and Row, 1966.
———. *The Long Revolution.* New York: Harper and Row, 1966.
Zeitlin, Irving M. *Marxism: A Reexamination.* New York: Van Nostrand Reinhold, 1967.

Articles

Bell, Daniel. "The Debate on Alienation," in *Revisionism: Essays in the History of Marxist Ideas.* Edited by Leopold Labedz. New York: Frederick Praeger, 1962.
Berland, Oscar. "Radical Chains: The Marxian Concept of Proletarian Mission," *Studies on the Left*, September-October 1966.
Bestor, E. "The Evolution of the Socialist Vocabulary," *Journal of the History of Ideas*, June 1948.
Briggs, Asa. "The Language of Class in Nineteenth Century England," in *Essays in Labour History.* Edited by Asa Briggs and John Saville. London: Macmillan, 1960.
Coornaert, E. "La pensée ouvrière et la conscience de classe: 1830-1848," in *Studi Onore di Gino Luzzato* 3. Milan: 1950.
Dos Santos, Theotonio. "The Concept of Social Classes," *Science and Society*, vol. 24, no. 2, summer 1970.
Johnson, Christopher H. "Communism and the Working Class before Marx," in *American Historical Review*, vol. 76, no. 3, June 1971.

Lehning, Arthur. "Buonarroti and his International Secret Societies," *International Review of Social History* 1, 1956, pp. 112-40.
——. "Buonarroti's Ideas on Communism and Dictatorship," *International Review of Social History* 2, 1957, pp. 266-87.
Lichtheim, George. "On the Interpretation of Marx's Thought," *Marxism and the Western World.* Edited by Nicholas Lobkowicz. Notre Dame, Ind.: University of Notre Dame Press, 1967.
Loubère, L. A. "The Intellectual Origins of French Jacobin Socialism," *International Review of Social History* 4, 1959.
Lubasz, Heinz. "Marx's Concept of the Revolutionary Proletariat," *Praxis,* vol. 5, no. 1-2, 1969.
Marcuse, Herbert. "The Obsolescence of Marxism," in *Marxism and the Western World.* Edited by Nicholas Lobkowicz. Notre Dame, Ind.: Notre Dame University Press, 1967.
Nicholaus, Martin, "Hegelian Choreography and the Capitalist Dialectic," *Studies on the Left,* November 1967.
——. "The Unknown Marx," *The New Left Review,* no. 48, March-April 1968.
Tönneson, K. D. "The Babouvists: From 'Utopian' to Practical Socialism," *Past and Present,* no. 22, July 1962.

Index

About the Author

Timothy McCarthy is associate professor of history at the University of Massachusetts at Boston. A specialist in the modern intellectual history of Europe, he has published articles in *Social Science*.